Praise for *Mountain Girl*

"This book about an indomitable woman offers hope for everything we want to believe about our country. Marilyn Moss Rockefeller proves that with courage, intelligence, and a sense of humor all things are possible."
　　　　　—Ruth Reichl, author of *Save Me the Plum*

"If there was ever a life worth writing about, it is Marilyn Moss Rockefeller's. *Mountain Girl* is her unassuming journey made epic by her capacity to find faith in her doubts; to own her struggles and triumphs; to be tenacious yet carefree; to crave adventure as well as stability; to ultimately say yes, yes, yes to all those moments—big and small—which make a life come alive."
　　　　　—Richard Blanco, author of *The Prince of Los Cocuyos*

"*Mountain Girl* is sometimes hilarious, sometimes tragic, sometimes jaw-dropping, and always a huge pleasure to read. Marilyn Moss Rockefeller's *Mountain Girl* is at once a classic American story and a delicious account of an off-the-charts life full of unpredictable turns."
　　　　　—Natalie Goldberg, author of *Writing Down the Bones*

"This is a book I will always treasure. Yes, it's a "rags to riches" narrative, but told by a woman with such honesty, insight, and evocative language that I didn't want to miss a single sentence."
　　　　　—Sena Jeter Naslund, author of *Ahab's Wife*

Mountain Girl

From Barefoot to Boardroom

Marilyn Moss Rockefeller

ISLANDPORT PRESS

ISLANDPORT PRESS

Islandport Press
PO Box 10
Yarmouth, Maine 04096
www.islandportpress.com

ISBN: 978-1-952143-48-9
Ebook ISBN: 978-1-952143-59-5
Library of Congress Control Number: 2022932247

Printed in the United States of America

Dean L. Lunt | Editor-in-Chief, Publisher
Genevieve A. Morgan | Senior Editor
Piper K. Wilber | Assistant Editor
Emily A. Lunt | Book Designer
Emily E. Boyer | Cover Designer

For Jeffrey, Genevieve, Pebble, and all my family.

Table of Contents

"The purpose of life, after all, is to live it, to taste experience to the utmost, to reach out eagerly and without fear for newer and richer experience."—Eleanor Roosevelt

Prologue

"I keep telling you, she's something else," Daddy said to his younger brother in his long, slow burn of a West Virginian accent. "She's a real pistol, and if she wants to shoot a gun, I'm gonna teach her."

It was October of 1946, and I was six years old. The three of us stood in Uncle Alex's field in West Virginia, no houses around for miles, a few faded orange and yellow leaves clinging to the naked trees.

"Ain't she too young for a gun, Charlie?" my Uncle Alex asked as he tipped the whiskey bottle back for another slug, then wiped his mouth with the back of his hand, stained black from working in the coal mine.

"Hell, no," Daddy said. "We learned to shoot a gun as soon as we could walk."

"Yeah, but we weren't no girls," Uncle Alex laughed and shook his head.

We could hear the noisy rush of the river where an occasional duck skidded across the water, then flapped its wings on its way to being airborne again. The sky was a clear, azure blue with a few bulbous clouds. Uncle Alex sat on a wooden keg by the old stone wall and lit a cigarette. Daddy squatted down beside me and placed the butt of the .22 rifle against my shoulder, then held the barrel for me. "You have to hold it up, sweetheart."

I was trying very hard. I wanted to make him proud of me. I had always thought my arms were strong, but the barrel continued to pitch down.

"Here, place your hand out here," he said gently. "Okay. Now, honey, I'm gonna help hold it the first time, 'til you get the feel of it."

Daddy reached to take the gun from me, stood up, and took off his suit jacket. He always wore a suit and tie when he wasn't driving heavy road machinery for the state of West Virginia. He folded his jacket carefully and hung it on a nearby tree limb, then loosened his tie and rolled up his white shirtsleeves.

I started to shake a little and wasn't sure whether I was excited or scared.

"You see that big can out there on the stone wall?" He pointed at a shiny metal can. "That's what you're gonna aim for. And you're gonna hit it."

I didn't feel nearly as confident as he sounded.

Daddy cocked open the barrel. Then, holding the rifle with his left hand, he put his right hand in his pocket, pulled out a cartridge, put it into the barrel, and snapped it shut. The metal-on-metal clang startled me. My knees started to shake and wouldn't stop. He squatted back down behind me, brought the rifle up to my shoulder, positioned my arms and hands, and placed my forefinger around the trigger. The barrel and trigger felt cold on my hands.

"Okay. You see the can?"

"Uh-huh."

He put his hand under the barrel to support it. "Now, move it gently to the left . . . then bring it to the right, back to the can."

I squeezed the trigger.

Nothing.

"Honey, you just didn't squeeze hard enough."

His index finger wrapped around mine on the trigger again.

Once again, I closed my left eye and lined up that little knob on the end of the gun with the can and repeated the movement of the rifle, left to right. Then I felt pressure from Daddy's finger on mine, and the gun fired.

I jumped back from the shove into my shoulder. "Did I hit it, Daddy?" I squealed.

"No, but that's okay," he said in his reassuring drawl, then patted my shoulder. "You're gonna get it all by yourself before the day's over." His face broke into his big, familiar smile.

That was all the encouragement I needed.

I'll keep trying until I knock that old can off the rocks.

Once more, he loaded the gun, put his arms around me, and squeezed my finger on the trigger. This time, when the gun fired, I was not so startled and tense. I still didn't hit the can, but Daddy kept smiling.

"Don'tcha give up. You almost got it." Then he gave me a hug and whispered the four familiar words: "You can do it. Say it, MarilynRae. Say 'I. Can. Do. It.'"

"I can do it. I can do it," I said, over and over.

I took aim and fired. Then again. My arm and shoulder ached. But damn, as Daddy would say, I was determined to do it.

With Daddy's hand gently on mine, I raised the rifle once again, took aim, and swung the rifle left to right until the can was inside the sight. Then I squeezed that trigger hard.

Plink. The can fell off the wall.

"I hit it!" I lowered the rifle, feeling like I'd burst with pride.

"Well, I'll be damned," Uncle Alex murmured, his cigarette bobbing up and down in his mouth. "I think you got that boy you wanted, you old coot."

Daddy smiled, lit a cigarette, and tossed his jacket over his shoulder with his right arm. Then he put his left hand on my shoulder and drew me close to him. "That's my girl."

Each time Daddy put the can back on the wall and reloaded the gun and I hit it, his smile stretched broader.

"I'm gonna do it again now, Daddy, all alone," I practically yelled.

Then I did it. Then I did it again.

My mother, my father, and me in Elgood, West Virginia, in 1945.

Chapter One
A Hillbilly Tomboy

"**M**arilynRae," my grandmother once said to me in our old farmhouse kitchen, while she poured hot water into a galvanized tub for my bath, "you're so feisty, I figure you're gonna be the president of the United States someday."

I told her I'd prefer to become a doctor. Doctors were the ones in the long white coats who gave me my polio vaccine. What did I know about presidents?

"Well, then, you be that." She smiled and tried to scrub more of the freckles off my cheeks with buttermilk.

Our farm was in a tiny, unincorporated town in West Virginia called Elgood, where I went barefoot every summer—climbing trees, milking cows, and shooting squirrels for breakfast with a .22 rifle. In many ways, the Nash family farm taught me everything I'd ever need to know about life—that it would require lots of hard work, equal amounts of humility, a little intuition, a great deal more listening, and, most of all, fearlessness. Again and again, during the good times and the hard times in my life, I've returned to that small Appalachian farm in my mind and to the strength and sense of wholeness I had there.

The story of my birth goes something like this: Not long after I'd arrived and the country doctor had left my parents' cramped, three-room, clapboard house in Bellepoint, West Virginia, my father took a drink from his whiskey bottle in the kitchen, took a puff on his cigarette, exhaled a long stream of smoke, and said, "Ray. It's Ray." Then he pulled himself up to his full six-foot-two-inch height and repeated it: "I like the name Ray." But Mom wanted to name me Marilyn. They couldn't agree. It would soon become a pattern.

Daddy had chosen my name several months earlier by relying on his Native American grandmother's fortune-telling. She'd never even met my mother, but after reading the lines in my father's palm, my 102-year-old great-grandma predicted her grandson would have a tall, strong boy. This was the same powerful woman who, four years later, held my own small hand in the air and announced, "This child is going to live—forever!" thereby instilling a belief in me that I could do absolutely anything I set out to do.

It wasn't until several days after my birth that Daddy finally went to the city courthouse to get my birth certificate. "MerlynRay McGraw" was the name that appeared on the document. Daddy's compromise. Mom later changed it to "MarilynRae McGraw. Female. January 28, 1940. Father: Charles William McGraw. Mother: Lucille Nash McGraw." No time of birth was recorded.

My parents met in 1937, after my father went on a date with one of my mother's sisters. Mom was a new graduate of Athens College, where she'd earned a two-year teaching certificate. The legend goes that Mom's sister brought her new beau home to meet the family—a tall, handsome, charismatic twenty-five-year-old in a suit and tie—and he was instantly attracted to my mother. His thick, black, wavy hair looked striking against his olive skin, and he walked with a swagger. Apparently, his soft voice and flirtatious black eyes caught Mom's attention. Daddy was the second youngest of thirteen and hadn't been schooled beyond eighth grade. He was all wrong for my eighteen-year-old mother. Of course, she fell wildly in love with him. When Mom's father announced that she was much too young to get engaged, they married secretly in 1938.

Very soon after my birth, Mom went back to teaching in a remote, one-room schoolhouse in Mercer County, while my father worked all over the state on construction crews. During the week, he'd rent rooms in boardinghouses and then meet up with my mother at her rental apartment on weekends. They couldn't possibly afford a babysitter, so Mom took me to school wrapped in blankets on the rear-window shelf of her Studebaker, where she could see me from her rearview

Me as a child in West Virginia in 1942.

mirror as she drove up and down the mountains. Muddy, deep-rutted roads in the fall and spring. Snow-covered and icy in the winter. Her younger brother Frankie has told me stories about her climbing out of her car to put chains on her tires to try another run at getting up a mountain in a snowstorm.

In my proudest memories, I carry an image of my five-foot-two mother dressed in a navy blue fitted suit-jacket and matching skirt with a cream-colored rayon blouse and high heels, braving the wind and snow to bend over each tire and perform the slow and tedious task of fastening the chains to the tires. She was unstoppable.

But the demands of a baby and long working hours began to wear on her, and she placed me in the loving care of her parents in Elgood, West Virginia, and that is where my story really begins.

My mother, father, and me in Bellepoint, West Virginia, in 1940.

Chapter Two

Little Behooves Any of Us to Find Fault in the Rest of Us

Elgood sat perched on a mountain in the southeast part of West Virginia, eight and a half miles from the Virginia border. At that time, the town consisted of one church with a cemetery, one schoolhouse for grades one through nine, and one general store with the town's only telephone. Three narrow roads twisted their way up the mountain's hairpin curves and converged in front of our farmhouse. Drivers blasted their horns before they rounded the tight corners, and the sound echoed to the farm's front porch where I sat in my favorite swing, hoping to see a car drive by.

The farmhouse itself was made of white wooden clapboards, with a small porch entry and two pillars in front that braced a little balcony. In the back, the land dropped abruptly into our holler, where my grandfather's cows roamed. The vegetable garden, chicken house, pigpen, and cow barn were carved out of a slightly flatter section of land along the road. A magnificent oak tree commanded the left side of our yard, with branches that reached up over the roof and were home to a big black racer snake. That snake and I stared one another down for hours whenever he coiled around the branch closest to my upstairs bedroom window.

My mother as a baby on Mom Nash's lap, with Dad Nash and one of her cousins in 1919.
—

Like most homes in those West Virginia mountains, we had an outhouse that sat on the edge of the backyard. I never understood why its door faced the road instead of the Blue Ridge Mountains, one of the most spectacular views around. On the other side of the yard stood the well pump and the clearing where a fire got built each fall to cook the apple butter. When it wasn't my turn to stir that delicious apple butter in the cast-iron kettle, I'd jump and hide in the big piles of leaves raked by my beloved maternal grandmother, Mom Nash. Born Sally Irene Neeley in 1896, Mom Nash was the soul of the farm. She raised me and was the one who taught me the power of patience and listening and how to keep my heart open.

Mom Nash and my grandfather, Dad Nash, were married in Pipestem, West Virginia, in 1918 and made a handsome couple— she was talkative and gregarious and sang and played a good guitar. Dad Nash, born Aubrey Roscoe Nash, was quiet and private and heir to the old Nash homestead. He was firm but gentle and didn't drink, smoke, or swear. He had little education and worked hard for the railroad when he wasn't at the farm, tending to the cows and butchering pigs to provide meat for the year. They had seven children, five girls and two boys, of which my mother was the eldest.

Mom once told me that when each child was born into the family after her, Dad Nash would wake my mom gently in the night and say, "Mommy's sick, and I have to get Dr. Vermillion. You take the children over to Grandma's for the rest of the night." He certainly never talked about where babies came from. He'd scoot her out the door to her grandparents' house across the field, then go to the barn, get on one horse, and trail another horse behind him seven miles to Dr. Vermillion's house to bring him back, many times during blizzards. When Mom and her siblings came home the next day, a new baby was there. Mom said it took her a few times to figure out what was happening.

Mom Nash loved to be on the move, cooking and cleaning and going anywhere she could get a ride—friends' houses, funerals, church services, quilting parties. She was the true center of town life and was even awarded the title of Farm Woman of the Year by the West Virginia Farm Bureau. Many days, I'd come home from school to find the living room filled with chattering women all hand-stitching a quilt stretched out on the wooden sawhorses. Mom Nash cut stacks and stacks of fabric squares from our old shirts and pajamas and nightgowns and aprons. Every bed in our farmhouse had at least one of her quilts on it, sometimes more, and I loved to study them and try to find my old clothes in the squares. If I snuck into the living room quietly and hid under the quilting frame, I could listen in on the gossip that wasn't meant for my young ears.

"Y'all hear about BettyLou? That no-good Jones man got her pregnant."

"Well, ain't that a pretty mess. What's she gonna do with a young'un? She's one herself."

"Well, I heard he isn't the one who done it."

"Well, I guess it could have been any of those boys she hangs out with."

Everyone would nod in agreement. Coffee pot on the stove in winter. Sugar-saturated iced tea in glass pitchers on the sideboard in summer. Each woman pitching in to make another quilt for the next needy family.

Cats, which seemed to multiply magically, were everywhere at the farm. Outside, that is. Animals weren't allowed in the house. Mom Nash called them "those wild cats" and claimed she didn't like them, although she put food scraps out in bowls for them every day.

"There goes one of them doggone cats," Dad Nash yelled as a cat ran across the yard. He hated them.

We had electricity, although it was often out of order, so kerosene lamps never left the tables. "You're gonna wreck your eyes with that kerosene light," Mom Nash warned me again and again. But I wasn't about to give up my reading at night, and to this day, I love the pungent smell of kerosene.

In the cold Appalachian winters, Mom Nash's warm kitchen summoned me. I spent as much time as I could in there, with the large, wood-burning cookstove that was never without a flame in its firebox. A cupboard and an iron sink with a hand pump competed for space. At some point in those first nine years of my life, running water magically materialized, along with an aluminum sink with faucets. But Mom Nash put up a fight against the electric stove for a good long time. "I just know it won't make good biscuits," she used to say in her West Virginian drawl. She finally relented, but she never fully trusted the new, fancy stove from Sears and Roebuck.

Her kitchen may have been the warmest room in the house, but the most warmth emanated from Mom Nash herself, always ready to give me a big hug. I loved the way she got up early each day, bathed, and put on a clean dress with earrings and a necklace, then tied a flowered, starched apron over the dress. Her hair was permed into small curls and neatly combed, and her nylon stockings sat rolled down to her ankles with her garters, ready to be pulled up at a moment's notice, her best shoes waiting side by side on the floor.

"Mom Nash," I'd ask her, "are you going somewhere today?"

She'd shake her head no. "I just want to be ready to hitch a ride if someone stops by on their way to Princeton."

Each morning in the predawn dark, I'd hear the sizzle of her fresh eggs and bacon. When I got downstairs, she'd greet me with, "MarilynRae, go wash your hands. Time to help make biscuits." Then she'd sit me on a pile of books on a chair and give me a small piece of dough to imitate her with. I loved the feel of that dough as I kneaded life into it. I didn't stray far from the kitchen until she brought the biscuits out of the oven and slathered the two halves with her homemade butter and huckleberry jam.

That biscuit was gone by the time she'd poured me a glass of milk.

"Don't put so much in your mouth at once or you'll choke," she'd tell me. "Remember Opal Thompson's boy, Eugene? He got a piece of potato stuck in his throat and died right there."

"Yes, ma'am," I'd manage.

I learned to make the biscuits and pies and cakes and cookies with Mom Nash. I learned to fry bacon and eggs and squirrel and pork. To chop off the heads of chickens and pick out their feathers and truss them for roasting. I learned to gather vegetables from the garden and fruit from our trees and bushes and to prepare it all for canning. When I wasn't in school, I spent Mondays in the root cellar with Mom Nash and her galvanized washtub. She washed the clothes and linens on the washboard, then fed them through the Sears and Roebuck wringer. My job was receiving and pulling them through. The whole time we were down there, when she wasn't making me recite multiplication tables or practice spelling words, she sang hymns from our church: "There's a church in the valley by the wildwood, no lovelier spot in the dale…" or "Onward Christian soldiers, marching as to war, with the cross of Jesus going on before…" I loved to sing along.

At one o'clock every Sunday, family and friends gathered at the farmhouse to feast. We were never quite sure who might show up, but the food and process of cooking it were absolute. Mom Nash started on Saturday, cutting off the heads of two or three of our chickens. I was meant to pick off their feathers while the chickens soaked. If it was summer, she'd harvest the vegetables—fresh tomatoes, carrots, potatoes, collards, green beans, onions, cabbage, shell beans, corn, spinach, peas, and cucumbers. If it was winter, she'd go down to the root cellar to get what she needed. Then she'd bake all the delicious fruit pies.

Each Sunday morning, she'd get out of bed at four sharp, put on her go-to-church dress, plus the ever-present necklace and earrings and an apron she'd made from grain bags, and then head to the kitchen to finish the remaining dishes before the service. When the last hymn got sung at church, she'd move quickly to shake hands with the preacher and make her exit, back to her kitchen.

Everyone would gather at our house directly after—all my aunts and uncles and cousins, plus my mother whenever she was visiting. If Mom was there, Sunday was the very best day, except when it was time for her to leave—and then I'd collapse in tears. Daddy never joined Sunday dinners, and I missed him keenly. I assumed he wasn't invited because Dad and Mom Nash didn't approve of his drinking or of his marrying Mom. On occasion, Mom Nash would invite the preacher of the day, contingent on a favorable sermon. And there was always the impromptu invitation to someone else who lived alone and looked as if he or she could use a good meal.

After church, it was impossible to keep me out of the trees with my cousins. I was alone all week on the farm with my grandparents, dreaming about having a bigger family—dreaming about my mother and my father and where they were each day without me—so having my cousins come on Sundays was gold. Finally, people my own age. Finally, some trees to climb and trouble to get into. I had to wear a dress to church, but that didn't stop me. Mom Nash knew I was the plucky ringleader and the first to get dirty. She'd lean out the kitchen screen door and yell, "MarilynRae! Don't get those kids up in any of them trees. Are you up in a tree? Y'all hear me?"

Of course, I was, but I had to scramble down the tree before I could answer her honestly. "No, ma'am. I'm not in a tree."

Promptly at one o'clock, someone would call, "Dinner's ready!" Then, all the men who'd been standing around on the porch or out in the yard looking under the hood of one of their cars would amble into the dining room and sit at the long, wooden table while the women stood behind them. Mom or Dad Nash would say grace unless the preacher was present.

This was back in the war years of the early 1940s, and hunger plagued most households around us. Unemployment was everywhere. Talk at the table was about the failing lumber industry and the mines producing too much coal and the textile mills closing. Isolated mountain towns like ours were affected the worst by the Depression, where it lasted longest, but you couldn't tell at our Sunday dinners because of how much work Mom Nash put into those meals.

After second helpings and the pies, the men would retire to the living room, where most succumbed to naps. This is when the women ate. After the men. It amazes me now, but that's the way it was back then. And after the women finished their meal, they'd sit around the table drinking coffee or iced tea and gossiping some more about who'd gotten engaged or gotten married or had a baby.

Sometimes, after the dishes got washed, one of my uncles would start playing a guitar or banjo and the others would join in singing, and this was my favorite thing. All the kids danced, and the day felt magical. I loved these Sundays in Elgood—Mom Nash's food, cooked with so much love, and our family rituals and togetherness. As an only child of two aging grandparents, I craved that Sunday family time, and I've carried the spirit of it with me ever since. In many ways, those Sundays on the farm showed me what real sharing means—and what opening up your home and feeding whoever is hungry looks like. It is something I've always tried to do, wherever I've been lucky to call home—keep an open door for whoever may need it and lots of good, home-cooked food on the table.

Our farmstead was, by most standards, impoverished, but I had no idea of this at the time because Mom and Dad Nash were so committed to providing food and love to everyone around them. I was surrounded by so much caring on that farm. A small, hand-stitched aphorism always hung in a frame over my grandparents' kitchen table:

THERE'S SO MUCH GOOD IN THE WORST OF US,
AND SO MUCH BAD IN THE BEST OF US,
THAT IT LITTLE BEHOOVES ANY OF US,
TO FIND FAULT IN THE REST OF US.

Back then, I'm not sure I knew what this saying really meant. But I now realize that my grandparents lived by these words. They were kind, giving people. Listeners instead of talkers. "Little behooves any of us, to find fault in the rest of us"—a saying that I would also come to live by.

My father in his Navy Construction Battalion, or "Seabees," uniform in 1942.

Chapter Three

A Dream Vanished

During World War II, my father served for two years as a
Seabee in the Navy, the military construction battalions
comprised of carpenters and engineers, masters of their
trades. The Seabees built bomber and fighter fields, seaplane bases,
ship-repair facilities, Quonset villages, hospitals, and the like in both
the Pacific and Atlantic theaters of operations. Their logo was the
Fighting Bee: "We build. We fight." As my father loved to tell me,
they had the "can-do" spirit. Daddy had long wished for a son, so
he later taught his daughter many tough "boy" things. All along, he
had me chanting, "I can do this. I can do this."

For a young child living in the mountains, the war was far
removed, except for the onion-skin letters with the strange-
looking stamps that came in the mail from Daddy. And Edward
R. Murrow's crackling evening news briefs on the wooden radio in
my grandparents' living room. "Be quiet, MarilynRae," Dad Nash
would warn me as he turned on the radio at the exact same time
each evening. Then he, Mom Nash, Uncle Frankie, and I sat close
to that brown wooden box, staring at it as if that would help us hear
better: "This is Edward Murrow, speaking from London."

Murrow reported from many different countries, following
what he called "Orchestrated Hell." Each night, he'd offer his closing
words: "Good night, and good luck." Then, Dad Nash would just

turn off the radio and go to bed. No explanation for his five-year-old granddaughter. I pieced together the horror of the war myself, and what I remember most was being scared for my daddy.

Meanwhile, my mother was teaching in a series of one-room schools throughout the state, eventually becoming the youngest—and the first female—superintendent of rural schools for West Virginia. She had progressive ideas for experiential learning in those tiny schoolhouses, first published in an article for the *West Virginia State Teachers' Magazine*. Her article garnered a great deal of attention and led to speaking engagements all around the state. Soon, she was organizing local parent–teacher associations. One of Mom's edicts was visiting the home of each one of her students, which she accomplished with the help of her trusted, secondhand, dark-blue Studebaker Commander, staying overnight if she had to.

Upon meeting Mom on the road, a local sheriff insisted on giving her a pistol. "A young woman shouldn't be driving alone in these rural areas without a gun," he told her.

Mom put the gun in the glove compartment. I think it reassured her, although as far as I know, she never used it. Perhaps the gun gave her the courage she needed to confront the farmer who wouldn't let his son attend school. Mom showed up at his farm to find out the reason for the boy's many absences, and the farmer threatened her with a shotgun. Mom stood there, hands on hips, and reminded the man of the law. Then she put her arm around the boy's shoulders and led him to the car, and off they drove.

At first she and Daddy took turns visiting me on Mom and Dad Nash's farm on sporadic weekends, but when I turned four, I started taking the train alone to visit them. Dad Nash called it "riding the rails." I loved it. Mom Nash would pin a tag with my mother's name and address on it to my coat. Then I'd climb aboard and sit in the caboose under the watchful eye of the conductor.

Around this time, the differences between my parents and their hopes and dreams were becoming a wedge. They argued about his drinking. They argued about money. They argued about where and when they could afford a place of their own together. But mostly, they argued about me.

Mom would correct my grammar, and then Daddy would swear at her for doing that. "Dammit, Lucille—I don't want my girl speaking like those smarty-pants snobs. She can say 'ain't' if she wants to. She's a mountain girl." Daddy also didn't like Mom's friends and would make fun of them, calling them "those fancy, high-falutin' teacher friends of yours."

When I turned six, they had the last fight that I remember.

It was a Saturday morning. I'd taken the train there by myself the day before for the weekend, and Mom was still in her pink nightgown and blue-flowered chenille robe, sitting at the kitchen table in her rented apartment. Her arms were folded tightly across her chest, like they always were when she was in serious conversation.

Daddy sat across from her, smoking one cigarette after another. He had on his blue-and-tan-striped pajamas with the top unbuttoned, revealing two tattoos, a bluebird on each side of his chest. A large glass ashtray with cigarette butts rested on the table by his coffee cup. Every now and then, Mom would fan the smoke away from her angry face with her hand.

I looked up occasionally, but I wasn't really listening to what they were saying. I was too busy paging through the book of paper clothes for my cardboard girl and boy paper dolls. But then my parents' voices became strident and loud.

"It was that damn nurse, wasn't it?" Mom said. I had never heard her swear before. "Charlie, I simply can't live like this anymore."

She got up from the table, carried her cup to the sink, and banged it into the metal dishpan. Tears slid down her cheeks. She paused and looked at me, then walked into the little side room she used as her office and sat down at her desk, her back to us.

The apartment became quiet. My body turned rigid.

Daddy took a few puffs on his cigarette, stubbed it out in the overflowing ashtray, then got up and walked into the bathroom off the kitchen. The door slammed. I heard running water and knew he was shaving, like he did every morning. But this morning, something was different—something bad.

Was this fight my fault? I tried to focus on cutting out the doll clothes from the book. After a short time, Daddy opened the bathroom door and walked into the bedroom. I stared at the cardboard girl's red-and-yellow-flowered bathing suit, carefully turning the paper with my left hand, making tiny scissor cuts with my right, so as not to make a mistake.

A few minutes later, Daddy came back into the kitchen, dressed in his gray suit, white shirt, and blue tie, carrying his worn tan suitcase. He put it down on the floor and poured another cup of coffee. Then he paused, looked at me, and let out a long sigh.

"C'mon, honey," he said in a soft, sweet voice, "Walk me to the car."

I jumped up and followed him in my pajamas.

"MarilynRae!" Mom yelled from the other room. "Don't go outside without your shoes and coat!"

I ran into the bedroom, pushed my feet into slippers, and grabbed my winter coat from the rack. I hurried outside and closed the apartment door behind me. Daddy had put his coffee cup on the ground by the curb and was opening the trunk of his blue Ford. He shoved his suitcase into the trunk and shut the lid. Then he sat in the driver's seat with his long legs and rested his feet on the curb. I ran to the car and stopped in front of him, my heart pounding into my ribs while my stomach churned. I willed tears not to form while I stood by the car door, waiting.

"Mommy and I can't live together no more."

He looked toward the apartment. Tears stung my cheeks and washed away a dream of a mommy and a daddy and a little girl in a small house with my own bedroom, a kitchen, and a puppy lying

My father sitting in the Studebaker in 1945.

in front of a fireplace, plus a fenced-in backyard with flowers, grass, trees, and a swing. These were the images I'd seen in picture books and dreamt about while lying alone in my bedroom at the farm.

"But don't go and worry none, honey," Daddy said. "I'm still gonna see you."

He reached slowly into his shirt pocket and took out a pack of Lucky Strikes. He shook out a cigarette and said, "Your mommy will put you on the train back to your grandma's, and I'll come get you soon for a weekend together." He raised the cigarette to his mouth, flipped open his Zippo lighter, and lit it. Then he looked at me with his dark eyes and inhaled. Long and deep. He slowly exhaled the stream of smoke, and his shoulders sank. The Zippo snapped shut, its metallic sound slicing through the quiet. "You be Daddy's good girl. And don't you forget I love you."

I started to cry harder.

23

He held open his arms and hugged me to his chest. The smell of his shaving lotion and coffee melted into me. "Daddy, please don't go," I cried between sobs. His heart thumped in my ear.

"You'll be fine, MarilynRae. I'll see you real soon. Be a big girl."

Chapter Four

Seabees Don't Die

Two years later, Mom Nash burst through the kitchen door at the farm, breathless.

"Honey," she said to me. "Your daddy's dead."

She'd just hurried back from the town telephone up at the general store, and she still had her apron on over her dress.

"Poor li'l MarilynRae," she said out loud to no one in particular. From this day forward, she would always use the "poor li'l" prefix before my name. She repeated it now: "Poor li'l MarilynRae."

"What do you mean?" I screamed at her as I sprang from my chair. "Daddy can't die. He's a Seabee!" Not my daddy, who was so tall, so strong, so handsome. Who drove those gigantic, crawling, clawing earth machines on the beaches of Okinawa.

But it was true. And several days later, Daddy lay in a glossy, pink casket inside the small, two-story house at the McGraw homestead in True, West Virginia, where he'd been born.

True was really in the middle of nowhere. It was a snowy, frigid December day, and sweat collected around the waistband of the too small wool skirt Mom had insisted I wear. My instinct was to bolt for the door. But I had to sit there like everybody else, staring at my daddy.

His arms were folded with his hands across his chest, and he wore his white shirt, the blue-and-gray-striped tie, and one of the two suits he owned. The room was packed with mourners who blocked the light from the one window in the small room. A stench of wet wool, mothballs, and sweat mingled with the sweet suffocating reek of carnations. All the while, a fiddle, a guitar, and a banjo slowly played "Nearer, My God, to Thee." A few people hummed along to the music.

When he'd come back to West Virginia after the war, Daddy had worked all over the state. His last job had been on the New River Gorge Bridge, then the world's longest single-span arch bridge, but it wasn't his dangerous work that had killed him. It was shaving at a small boardinghouse in the town of Gauley Bridge. The shared bathroom had a slow gas leak. The sign reading GAS LEAK— LEAVE WINDOW OPEN had fallen behind the heater. The window was closed, and he was asphyxiated. The landlady had found him slumped over the rim of the tub, at the age of thirty-five, his hand still holding the razor.

I looked at his motionless face in the casket, then looked away. *He was really gone. But was he still watching me?*

The putrid smell from the wilting carnations filled my nostrils and banged into the back of my head, returning me back to the room, back to the casket. I looked at his white face again. What was that awful white powder covering Daddy's face? It made him look like Maxine, the waitress at the lunch counter at the five-and-dime store in Princeton. One time, we were in there, and Mom Nash had whispered in my ear, "Don't you ever put that stuff on your face."

Why did they make Daddy look like that?

I had so many questions, but I didn't dare speak.

Suddenly, one of the women lifted me off the couch, carried me over to the casket, lowered me down, and said, "Give your daddy his last kiss." I clung to her dress while she tried to push me closer to his face. "MarilynRae," she said sternly now. "Your daddy would want you to kiss him good-bye."

I held my breath, then curled my lips into my teeth so they barely touched Daddy's cold skin before I jerked them away as nausea rose in my chest. The woman tried again, holding me with one arm and trying to pry my hands loose from her dress. But I clung even harder. She finally turned and dropped me back on the couch to resume the vigil.

Mom looked like she was going to burst into tears.

Daddy, get us out of here! I yelled silently.

When we got back to the farm, Mom Nash placed a biscuit slathered with butter and jam on my plate and said, "I need sugar for that apple pie I promised to make you. Why don't you get on over to the store and get a small bag for me?"

I knew she was trying to raise my spirits.

I liked going to Ray's. The store was a wonderland. Two-storied and wood-framed, it was planted across from the elementary school, half-tucked into the side of the hill. Inside were stacks of canned foods and burlap bags of grain and barley and white rice and flour. Plus, women's silk stockings, farm tools, men's coveralls, work boots, and socks. Best of all were the penny horehound drops and the root beer and Pepsi in thick, clear glass bottles, six for a dollar. I felt so grown up going there by myself. Ray called me "Li'l Sunshine." I called him Ray.

In good weather, the area's old, wrinkled men rolled their tobacco in thin white sheets of cigarette paper on the store's porch. In the winter, they gathered inside around the cast-iron, potbellied coal stove. There was the occasional spitting and spattering of tobacco chew, providing a good reason to remember to wear my shoes. The men talked of who was sick in town, who'd died, who'd had a baby, who'd been "foolin' around." Ray knew everything going on for miles.

Normally, he and the men kindly teased me: "Whatcha gonna do with that corn meal, MarilynRae, make some cornbread for your granddaddy?"

"She'd climb a tree instead of cookin'," another man might add.

"I think she's part monkey," someone else might say.

He was probably right there. I loved to climb trees, the higher, the better.

"MarilynRae, you get a squirrel yet this mornin'?" someone else might ask, laughing.

I could never understand why that was so funny, since my uncle Frankie and I often shot squirrels for Mom Nash to cook for our breakfast. But that day, after seeing Daddy in his pink casket, there wasn't any teasing, only tipped hats and mumbled condolences.

Ray asked me his usual: "Your granny want this on the credit slip?" And, as usual, he tucked a piece of hard candy in my hand. "Sorry about your daddy." The silence was heavy on my head and shoulders as he gave me the bag of sugar and an extra piece of candy. "Y'all take care yourself, Li'l Sunshine, you hear?"

When I left the store, nausea churned in my stomach again. I turned and looked at the church at the top of the hill—a simple, white clapboard building, steepled, with a bell that could be heard ringing for Sunday service all over the hollers. Normally, I had an aversion to that church, so grim and stern, with such solemn music and a preacher who yelled at us about how sinful we were, headed for damnation. But I ran to that church now for some reason, cradling the bag of sugar, stopping only when I reached the front door, which was always unlocked.

Cold and dampness hit me as soon as I entered. I still don't know why I sought out that dark church as my sanctuary that day. Maybe it was because of a memory I carried with me of a different, much more joyful church—the Black church I'd hitchhiked to by myself a couple years before. I had happened to see a group of Black men and women come up the road headed for Ray's store one day, singing "This little light of mine, I'm gonna let it shine, let it shine, let it shine, let it shine." Their voices were strong and full of emotion, and many of the people were dancing and clapping their hands. When they got closer to the store, I called out to them, "I like your singing! Can I hear more?"

"You can come to our church and hear more," one of the women yelled. "Every Sunday, young lady."

Not long after that, I'd hatched a plan and told a lie to Mom Nash so I could slip away from the farm to go find that church with all its joy and singing. I still regret lying to Mom Nash, because I had never lied to her before, but I do not regret going to the church.

It was a hot Sunday in June, and I walked along the dusty road until a kind couple on their own way to the church stopped their truck for me. When we got there, the woman, whose name was Beulah, took my hand and led me inside and seated me next to her. The rest was magic. So much singing and clapping. No solemn, out-of-tune piano. No preacher telling us all that we were all damned and going to Hell, like the preacher back at the church in Elgood. No, this new preacher talked about the glory land, and each time he did, "Hallelujahs" burst forth from the congregation. To me, it felt like a happy place. Not at all like the cold church in Elgood where I found myself sitting now. A shiver ran through my body then, and I had to get out.

I closed the door behind me and headed back down the hill to the farm. I could hear my daddy's voice in my head now and see his face as I walked—it was our last Christmas together, and we were at my Aunt Lottie and Uncle Frank's. Daddy was dressed in the same gray suit, white shirt, and striped tie he wore in the casket, and Aunt Lottie had decorated her front door with Christmas bells that jingled as we went inside. My eyes shifted right away to a shiny, blue-and-white girl's bike, complete with foxtails hanging from the white rubber handlebars. I squealed and ran first to the bike, then back to hug Daddy's legs, then back to the bike again.

"Is it really mine?" I couldn't believe it.

"It's really all yours, honey," Daddy said. "It's for Daddy's girl."

It didn't take long for me to drag him and my new bike outside. I was determined to ride it, even though the bike now appeared so much larger than me.

"Stand on the pedals," Daddy said gently. "I'll hold it 'til you get the hang of it. You'll ride this damn thing today. You can do it, MarilynRae. Say it."

"I. Can. Do. It. I. Can. Do. It!" I yelled.

My heart was racing. It was a cold day, and the street was wet from a recent snow. I hadn't taken the time to put my sweater back on, and I could feel goosebumps crawling on my legs and arms. But Daddy was running alongside me now, with his right hand holding the bike seat and his left gripping the handlebar.

"Don't let go, Daddy!" I yelled while my hair blew around my face. The thrill of riding was like climbing to the top of the highest tree at the farm, but even better. "Where are you, Daddy?" I screamed, not daring to look back for him and risk losing my balance. "I'm scared!"

"I'm right here, MarilynRae. You're doing great. That's my girl!"

Chapter Five

Elbows Off the Table:
The Obliteration of Li'l MarilynRae

Not long after Daddy died, my mother moved north across the Mason–Dixon Line, and I left the farm to join her for good. Mom and Dad Nash drove me the seventeen miles to the train station. It was a long, sad, quiet drive. Although I didn't know it then, this drive marked a turning point in my life. I was leaving the farm. Leaving the little girl I was behind and becoming someone entirely new.

When we got to the station, Mom Nash gave the porter her instructions one last time: "Now you all take good care of my granddaughter, you hear?" Then she pinned her note to my dress with her neat handwriting: "MarilynRae McGraw. In case of accident, notify her mother—Lucille Nash McGraw." This was embarrassing. At nine years old, I didn't think I needed a child's tag any longer. But when Mom Nash hugged me one last time, I saw tears in her eyes, which caused me to cry.

"Y'all take care, MarilynRae," she said. "And be good for your mommy."

Dad Nash looked at me. "Don't you become one of them darn Yankees."

Then the porter took my hand and pulled me up the steps.

"All aboard!"

The sound of my beating heart competed with the metallic click of the wheels on the rails as I settled into the soft upholstered seat. I had on the new, blue-checkered dress Mom Nash had made from the fabric she'd bought in Princeton instead of the flour and grain bags she usually used. I felt so grown-up and alone on that train.

I stared out the window with my two dark braids hanging down my shoulders. I was nervous to see my mother. I'd never figured out what to expect with her. Sometimes it felt like she didn't know me—or didn't know the scrappy tomboy I'd turned into on the farm. And Mom had moved to so many different towns over the years, sometimes I felt like I hardly knew her, either. Now I was going to *live* with her?

A few hours later, the porter touched my shoulder to wake me.

"Better get ready, Miss MarilynRae. Baltimore's the next stop, and you're going to see your mommy."

Butterflies swirled in my stomach. I was getting worried. I'd been waiting for this moment for years, but now I had no idea what I was getting into. *Am I going to be happy living with Mom? What is this new life of mine going to be like?*

If only I'd known that it would require a full reinvention of myself.

Then, there she was, waiting on the platform as the train pulled to a stop. She looked so beautiful in her smart gray coat, its fur collar framing her smiling face. I felt much better, just seeing her. I jumped down the steps, and she gave me a rare hug and unpinned Mom Nash's note from my coat. Then she said the words I'd been waiting to hear her say my entire life: "Let's go home." I wasn't prepared, however, for what Mom's version of *home* meant.

It started with the actual apartment. Wow. All her hard, hard work had begun paying off, and her fortune had finally changed. This latest rental was on the third floor of a large apartment complex, and it had a big combined living and dining room, a separate modern kitchen, plus two big bedrooms with a bathroom in between. I couldn't believe it. She'd never lived in anything so grand as this.

"Here's your bedroom," she said, leading the way down the little hall to a room with twin maple beds, covered with pink-flowered bedspreads.

"It's beautiful," I blurted out, bouncing on the bed. "Who's going to stay in the other bedroom?" In Mom's West Virginia rentals, we'd always shared a bed, so I assumed she'd sleep with me in one of the twins. That was what I wanted most of all—to be near Mom at night, to share a room, and my secrets, with her.

"I was waiting until you were here with me to tell you." She smiled. "Arnie and I are planning to get married in three months. He'll be moving in here with us. You do remember him, don't you?"

I vaguely remembered meeting a man named Arnie . . . but marriage? It all seemed so sudden. I'd been fantasizing for so long about living *alone* with Mom. We were finally going to get to know one another because, in many ways, we were strangers. Living with Arnie was not at all what I'd expected. In fact, nothing in Maryland was what I expected.

So much of Mom's new world felt foreign to me. The people here talked differently and sounded odd. The clothes were all different, too. For starters, I was hardly ever allowed to wear my blue jeans anymore, which felt like an affront to my senses. The houses were not the same, either—so many apartment buildings and parking lots. Where was the big oak tree for my friend, the black racer snake? Where was the pigpen and the cow barn? Even my mother seemed different than I remembered. Stricter. Less forgiving. She said I was no longer MarilynRae. I was simply Marilyn. Mom dropped the "Rae"—too Southern, she said. But inside, I was still the tree-climbing tomboy from the mountains, and this new identity was totally confusing. *Who am I now, really?*

"Elbows off the table, Marilyn," Mom told me that first evening in Maryland, after she placed a bowl with Dinty Moore Beef Stew on the table. "And sit up straight. Manners are very important. I don't want you to forget that, no matter where you are or with whom. And tomorrow, we simply must do something with your hair. You're too old to still be wearing braids."

The next morning, she took me to a salon for a haircut and a perm. This was only the beginning. At every dinner, and sometimes at breakfast, Mom worked hard at my transformation. No easy task, given that I was a Southern mountain hillbilly. But Mom was determined. She drilled me on my manners, correcting me on how I held my knife and fork. "You always put your napkin on your lap as soon as you sit down at the table," she said, "gracefully."

She made me practice walking, shoulders back, with a dictionary on my head, and she taught me to sit properly, "like a lady." Knees together or tightly crossed, or legs crossed at the ankles, hands cupped on my lap. She bought me skirts and blouses and sweaters. My beloved jeans were only for softball games on Sundays or the rare occasion when we went camping.

I started to worry that Mom Nash and Dad Nash and my school friends back in Elgood would no longer recognize me. Maybe they wouldn't even *like* me anymore. I kept wondering— was I now one of those "*damn* Yankees" that Dad Nash warned me about? I was losing MarilynRae. But who was I becoming? I had no idea. It took me a long time to figure out the answer.

Mom's biggest obstacle, and my hardest challenge yet, was to drop my accent. I had no idea that I spoke "funny." But Mom said I needed to change how I talked if I didn't want to be teased by the other kids. And sure enough, when I started at my first school in Maryland, the kids made fun of me.

Night after night, Mom and I sat across from one another at supper, and she insisted that I practice: "How. Now. Brown. Cow." We did it over and over. The phrase had to be enunciated articulately and slowly, with my lips rounded out and puckered around the "o." The suppertime sessions got more and more painful, because I could hear all the other kids playing outside. Mom just closed the window.

"Concentrate, Marilyn," she'd say. "Or you'll never change. Repeat after me: 'How . . . now . . . brown . . . cow'." I watched her pinch and pucker her red lips, slowly opening and closing them around the vowels. Then she scrunched up her lovely face and protruded her lips, resembling a gasping fish.

At first, no matter how hard I tried rounding and puckering my lips, they slid back toward my ears: "Hal, nal, bran, cal." No resemblance to Mom's soft, melodious tones.

Mom grimaced.

I sighed.

But gradually, my hillbilly accent faded.

In many ways, Mom was more like my older sister than my mother. Her hugs were stiff and fleeting, and I don't remember her ever kissing me once, even before she moved north. One day in Maryland, she painted my toenails, and even though I loved it, I told her, "Mom Nash says only tacky girls wear nail polish, and the preacher yelled at all us girls, saying that if we ever wore polish, we'd go straight to Hell."

"Well, Mom Nash won't know, will she?" Mom said. "And we won't tell her."

Mom treated me as if I were much older than I was, and I took this as a sign of approval, but I also sorely missed being a little girl on the farm. I missed my grandmother's soft lap and her hugs and kisses. The warmth of her old kitchen, the smells of her cooking, the farm animals, and the big yard with good trees to climb. I was learning to become someone entirely new with Mom. A proper girl named Marilyn. Someone who talked differently and walked differently and was on a crash course to learn how to fit in.

Mom's hard-and-fast rule was that I had to do my homework alone at the dining table in the apartment until she got back from work. But after I'd been in Maryland about two months, I kept seeing my new friends playing in the apartment building parking lot. One day, I was extra bored and convinced myself that it was *only* the parking lot. I'd just play for a *few minutes*, then come back inside before Mom got home.

There was a chill in the November air, so I put my cardigan on over my blouse but didn't take the time to change from my shorts to long pants, which would prove to be a mistake.

"C'mon, Marilyn!" a friend yelled once I got down to the parking lot. "Loretta is 'it'!"

Daylight was fading, and it was hard to see. I swerved around one car and caught my leg on the fender. A burning sensation crawled up my leg instantly.

"Time-out!" I yelled and limped over to the entrance of our building. The whole gang stood around me under the outside light, where it was easy to see the two- to three-inch cut in my leg and the blood flowing down into my shoe.

"Yegads, Marilyn!" Loretta said. "That looks awful! You better get to a doctor. I'll go find my mom."

"No, no." I tried to remain calm. "Don't tell your mom. She'll tell my mom, and I'm not supposed to be out here. I gotta go."

I took off my sweater and wrapped it around my leg, tying the sleeves together to hold it in place. Then I climbed the fire-escape stairs to our third-floor apartment and hobbled into the bathroom. *What a mess I'm in this time. I have to fix my leg and soon. What if Mom comes back now?*

I kicked off my shoes and sat on the edge of the tub, washing my leg off with the running water. Somewhere I'd heard that putting pressure on a cut would stop the bleeding, so I pushed the sides of the cut together and pressed hard with a washcloth. But when I lifted it off, the sides of the cut opened up, and the bleeding started again.

"Well, I guess I need to sew it up," I said out loud, to induce courage.

Mom's sewing basket was in the bedroom. The trick was to keep from dripping more blood on the floor while I walked in there to get the basket. I took out a needle and debated over what color thread to use. "White seems the best," I said, to no one, again.

Back in the bathroom, I took out a bottle of rubbing alcohol and dribbled some on the cut to numb it. "Yeow!" Tears stung my eyes. Then I pushed the sides of the cut together again and took a deep breath. "Here goes!"

It really wasn't so bad, not as bad as I thought it would be, and my stitching handiwork even looked pretty secure. I cleaned up the mess and hid my sweater in the trash bin outside. By now, I'd started shaking, but I'd solved my problem on my own, addressed my own predicament. Luckily, the wound didn't get infected, and Mom never found it. I insisted on wearing long pants for the next few weeks before I removed the stitches with her cuticle cutter. I had taken care of myself like a real grown-up. I didn't need my mother to help me.

In many ways, fixing the gash on my leg was a precursor to the next muddled stage of my life—I had independence now. I had my own inner resolve. My own stubborn strength. But I also had the new skill that Mom had instilled within me—a strong talent for "pleasing" and shapeshifting. I was forever trying to become the girl that Mom most wanted me to be. Her new schooling was both a gift and a curse, because in my experience, we can only please others for so long before the acting takes its toll, and you begin to crave authenticity—to be who you really are.

Chapter Six

But Who Is She?

When Mom's new husband, Arnie—also a teacher, like her—moved into the house, he treated me like an adult, just like Mom did. Arnie introduced me to classical music and poetry and astronomy. "Marilyn," he'd say as he headed to the front door, "this is a great night to observe the eastern sky." I'd be right behind him. I loved to hear him tell of how Orion the Hunter and Perseus killed Medusa, which freed the beautiful Pegasus. Inside the house, Arnie played his favorite operas on the record player and recounted the stories of each production to me. He was intelligent, amusing, and affable. My mother and I soon learned he was also an alcoholic.

Slowly, the signs became more noticeable. Arnie would turn moody and irritable, especially when there was any talk of his daughter, who was the same age as me and lived with his ex-wife. He started leaving our apartment right after dinner, saying he was going to a "practice" with his opera group. Or that he had to go back to school and grade papers. Or that he had a meeting with the parents of a troubled student.

One evening, on his daughter's birthday, he didn't come home for dinner at all. Mom called around to see if anyone knew anything, but eventually we both went to bed. Around two in the morning, the phone rang. Mom grabbed the receiver, while I stood by her side, listening in as best I could.

"Is this Mrs. Richmond?" I heard a male voice say, and then ". . . fortunately, he didn't hurt himself or anyone else. We pulled him over before something terrible happened. He'll have to appear in court. And the car needs to be towed."

The idyllic family scenes I'd been building up in my mind again—the evening dinners and picnics in the country, the operas and concerts in Washington, DC—all soon vanished as alcoholism consumed Arnie. Thankfully, he wasn't an angry drunk. He just curled up in a knot on the couch and slept it off. Mom enlisted my help to beg him to go to rehab for the sake of the whole family. Arnie would hug us both and swear to stop drinking. But he never did. By the end of my first year in Maryland, he'd lost his job, then his singing voice, then his driver's license, and then his opera gig. Mom started hiding the keys to the cars, hiding his shoes, and begging him to stay in the apartment, all to keep him from going out drinking.

One night, long after dinner, I heard Mom and Arnie arguing, and I got up from my desk to close my door. I saw a scene that froze me in place. My five-foot-two mother was sitting in a chair she'd dragged in front of our entrance door, while Arnie stood a few feet away, wearing his suit jacket over his pajamas, with socks on but no shoes. Mom was pointing a large kitchen knife at him and yelling, "You are not getting through that goddamn door!"

Then she turned and looked straight at me. "Marilyn, get my car keys from the counter—*now!*"

I hurried into the kitchen, grabbed her keys, and put them in my pocket.

"Lucille," Arnie said to Mom. "That's a big knife for a small lady. You wouldn't really hurt me, would you?"

"Just you try me. I'm sick and tired of it. If you don't get help, we're finished."

I had never seen my mother so mad.

He headed into my bedroom, then closed the door behind him. I heard the lock click.

It took a while for Mom to calm down and find the key to the door, and when we opened it, he was gone. He'd escaped through my third-floor window by tying the sheets together and attaching one end to my bed. Snow blew into the room through the open window.

My mother sitting on the trunk of the Studebaker in 1945.

A few days later, Mom and I packed up and moved on to yet another new apartment in yet another new neighborhood to start yet another new life. Each beginning took me further and further away from my Appalachian Mountains.

In June, I finally got to take the train back to the farm in Elgood for the summer. I was elated. There I was again, sitting in the old, squeaky swing. Not simply any swing. A weathered, wooden-slatted swing with a back and arms that hung by four rusty chains. My swing. My happy place. How I had loved to sit and swing in the silence of the hot summer days with their heavy air. To hear the squeaking of the swing and the drone of the bees lazily buzzing, the birds too hot to sing. I'd spent hours in this swing, straining to hear a car engine winding up from the hollers. Why did I feel so strange being back there now?

Everything looked the same at the farm. Maybe a few more cars passed by, and the old house across the street had been torn down, and our yard fence had been repaired.

Me. That's what had changed. Me.

My mother had changed my hair and put me in frilly dresses and fancy shoes. Worst of all, her attempt to rid me of my mountain accent had left me garbling out some strange new foreign language. It's a wonder anyone could understand me. At least, Mom and Dad Nash still called me MarilynRae. But my mother had made it very clear: I was no longer a tomboy. No longer "li'l MarilynRae." I was Marilyn now.

But who was Marilyn? I really had no idea. My heart and soul were rooted at the farm, but Mom had a brand-new map and entirely different plans for me. She was pulling me north, in a whole new direction, and I could only follow.

Chapter Seven

Being a Chameleon
in a Peripatetic Life

M om and I kept migrating north from job to job. School to school. Town to town. Apartment to apartment. She was climbing up the career ladder. I was changing schools, often in the middle of the year, and trying to make new friends each time. It was like nothing I had ever imagined after nine years living at the top of that small mountain in Appalachia. Our lives had become peripatetic now. Sometimes, we moved two or three times in the same state. All I could do was try to fit in. Try to please whomever I could.

"Please welcome Marilyn to our school," one principal after another said to a classroom of expressionless faces as I stood awkwardly at the front of the class.

The more Mom and I moved, the more I learned about how to be a chameleon—to walk with poise into a new homeroom in the middle of a school year. To listen and shapeshift. I attended the Catholic church with my Italian and Irish friends. Visited the synagogue with my Jewish friends. Spaghetti became pasta. I overcame my doubt that gefilte fish was really fish. Meat and potato dishes became Irish stew. Lox and bagels replaced scrambled eggs for breakfast. I learned what the expressions *Kish mir in tuchas* and *stunad* meant. I danced to their music, played the required parts. It always seemed like I was acting, trying on disguises, moving with an automaton button turned on.

I wanted to be liked by everyone, but pleasing my mother was still foremost. And it was difficult. It took a toll on me that I could not yet begin to measure, the need to please her.

This was the time in my life when I really began trying to find myself through the eyes of others, and I lost touch with my own feelings and needs. I put li'l MarilynRae in a room at the farm and closed the door on her for a very long time.

When Mom rented a small house in Vernon, Connecticut, from a dairy farmer named Bill Randall, the place felt like a palace—two small bedrooms upstairs with a bathroom, plus a kitchen and living room and another half-bath downstairs. There was even a yard outside with trees and flowering shrubs, and Bill Randall himself supplied us with fresh vegetables, milk, eggs, and strawberries from his farm—his gentle way of courting Mom. It worked, although only for a while.

But before Mom and I left Vernon, Bill Randall asked me one of the most important questions I've ever been asked in my life. I was doing homework after dinner at the kitchen table when he took the chair next to me and said, out of nowhere, "What's your passion?"

His handsome face was tanned and rutted from all the hard farm work, and I could tell how serious he was from his tone. His words still resonate with me now: "You're one of the strongest thirteen-year-olds I know. Boys included. But what do you want to be when you grow up?"

I prided myself on being strong, and I could beat all the boys in my class in arm-wrestling. But my *passion*? I didn't know what he was talking about.

"What do you mean?"

I'll never forget what he said next.

"Well, what do you like to do the most, or what do you want to do when you become an adult?" His voice conveyed gentleness. "You know, what do you want to do after you finish college?"

I still dreamed of becoming a doctor.

"Oh, maybe I could be a doctor," I said. "Also, I like music . . . and dancing. I love reading and writing in my diary . . . I guess I don't know. I just want to please Mom."

Bill looked at me strangely. "Well, you don't have to make up your mind this soon. You have lots of time. And you should do what gives *you* satisfaction."

I stared at him and really took his words in. What gives *me* satisfaction? I almost couldn't grasp what he meant. But I knew there was some elemental truth in what he'd said. Some real wisdom. It took me a long time to understand him—that life did not have to mean pleasing others. That I could carve my own path and lead in my own way. It would take years. Decades. But by trial and error and many fits and starts, I'd eventually get there. I would run my own company and lead it with heart and soul—just like Mom Nash ran her farmhouse.

Mom and I moved again. And then again.

When I was fifteen, she married a man named Seward Beacom, and the moving finally stopped. "Beac" was a college chemistry professor, divorced, with no children, and early on, I heard him say, "I won Lucille over at a college faculty dinner dance by cutting in as she was dancing with a drunken colleague. But I still had to win the approval of Marilyn."

The first time he came to dinner, I was cramming for a high school chemistry test, and he pulled out the chair at the dining table and sat down in his blue suit and red-and-blue bow tie and said, "Since I teach chemistry, maybe I can help you." I turned the book toward him. He worked with me for hours before and after dinner, and in this way, he won me over.

Here I am after being crowned New Britain High School's homecoming queen in Connecticut in 1956.

I gave the two-thumbs-up signal to my mother the next morning, and soon after that, we moved into Beac's house in New Britain, Connecticut, where he introduced me to his strict rubric of rules—curfew must be adhered to, or no more dates were allowed. All school dances must have chaperones. Grades were not to drop below a B, and only one B was acceptable per semester. Now I tried hard to be perfect at everything in high school. To be the *best*. At least, in Mom's—and now Beac's—eyes.

You name it, I tried it. I was elected class president and homecoming queen, plus prom queen and Girls State representative in the American Legion Auxiliary's Connecticut government program. I was inducted into the National Honor Society and was selected for the Daughters of the American Revolution Good Citizenship Scholarship. I had many boyfriends and exchanged secrets with my girlfriends. I exalted over crushes and cried dramatically over heartbreak into my pillow.

But it seemed like I was acting all the time now, moving through life with that automaton button still stuck on.

Mom kept a photo of me as homecoming queen, riding on the back of a convertible, gowned in chiffon, roses in my arms. The truth was, I didn't know the real me. Sometimes I felt so alone and scared and incapable—I don't think I had a clue what I was doing. I was just responding to what I thought people *wanted* me to do and wanted me to be.

And I was lonely.

Chapter Eight

Rebel

In 1957, I enrolled in a small Midwestern college—Beac's choice not mine—with the intention to become a doctor. I had the grades and the ambition, at least for the first two years. Then, at the start of my junior year, I nominated my roommate Rebecca for membership to my sorority. I hadn't even known what a sorority was when I got to campus, and I only joined one because all my roommates were doing it. I was guilty of still very much wanting to fit in.

"I nominate Rebecca Bailey," I said to the group of girls at the sorority house when it came my turn to speak. "I think most of you know her. She's my roommate this year, so I've had the opportunity to get to know her well." Here, I paused.

My sorority sisters were fidgeting and turning and looking at one another.

"She meets all of our requirements," I said, "excellent grades, active in sports and other extracurricular activities, wonderful personality—"

I was cut off by the president of the sorority. "Marilyn, uh . . . we can't . . . she can't . . . I thought you would know that you can't nominate her."

"Why not?" I asked in the calmest voice I could manage. "She qualifies as much as anyone else who's been nominated."

The president focused her eyes on the floor, not on me. "The sorority does not accept any coloreds."

"What?" I nearly yelled. "That's absurd. Unfair. And no, I didn't know." I was using my loud voice. "If I had known, I wouldn't have joined in the first place!"

I quickly undid my sorority pin from my sweater and threw it on the floor. "If you don't want Rebecca, then I don't want you!" Then I moved calmly through all the shocked faces and out the door.

It didn't take long for the news to travel around campus, eventually reaching the office of the college president, who called me in the next morning.

"Marilyn," he said sternly, "I think you may need a little rest from school. I have phoned your folks. They're coming to get you. I'm sorry I have to do this, but you can apply to come back next semester. I'm sure you understand why."

"No, sir. I don't."

Sitting in my dorm room that evening, I told Rebecca the whole chain of events. She was horrified, claiming she was just one of the school's "tokens."

"Of course they wouldn't accept me," she said. "I wish you'd told me what you were going to do, and I could have warned you." She started to cry. "You're the only friend I have here. Everyone else has to struggle just to smile at me."

At home, I was ashamed of my naiveté and of putting Rebecca in such a terrible, exposed position. I soon received a letter from her stating that she, too, had left the school. I became more and more depressed. I had finally stopped trying to please everyone. I'd finally gotten stubborn and pushed back, and look where it had gotten me and Rebecca.

Beac suggested I transfer to the University of Michigan in Ann Arbor, where he'd received his doctorate, and soon after, I moved into a tiny, single room in an old stone dormitory there. The austerity of that place seemed fitting for my keen disillusionment. The room consisted of a twin bed crammed in the corner, a small closet, a chair and table for a desk, and a little sink.

I loved it. I was finally alone, just like I'd been on the farm in Elgood. For the first time in years, I didn't have to fit in or try to please anyone. I could just curl up on my bed, read voraciously, and listen to albums on my phonograph. It was a huge shift for me. No one forced me to put on a costume. No one demanded that I perform for them.

I finally began to listen to the quiet voice inside of me. I didn't succumb to any peer pressure to join another sorority. I wore the clothes that I wanted to. Listened to the music that I liked. Stayed up all night reading if it suited me. Never had I been given this kind of time to spend with myself. In the evenings, I gravitated toward activist group meetings in the student hall. And as I read more books on slavery and on the Holocaust, I became angrier at the pervasive racism I could see all around me.

I started skipping classes. I didn't feel the need to study anymore. What was the use? It was a radical change in me. For so long, I had tried to be the good girl. For so long, I had tried to be the perfect daughter for my mother. Tried to be Marilyn, who did not talk funny and did not climb proverbial trees. But the acting job had become exhausting. The automaton couldn't do it anymore. Her shelf life had run out. Besides, it didn't make sense to study chemistry when so much was wrong in the universe. It seemed, in many ways, that I wanted to punish myself for what had happened with Rebecca. I blamed my college sorority. I blamed the college president. Mostly, I blamed myself for not understanding the scope of the racism that Rebecca was up against.

Meanwhile, I wrote to Mom and Beac that everything was great: "I am doing well in classes, I have many friends . . . and, of course, I love U of M and attend the football games on Saturdays." All lies.

My grades were dropping. My mother suggested that at least I should get a teaching degree, and as part of my new child development program, I spent one summer in Michigan working at a camp for troubled youth, ages five to sixteen. A lot of the kids came from poor, Black neighborhoods, where the wage gap between the children's families and the wealthier kids at the university was enormous. I became totally absorbed in my work with these kids, and it slowly brought me out of my cocoon and out of my head, back into the world with all its inequity. Now I felt like I had purpose.

My last year of college, I got a part-time job as a receptionist and bookkeeper at a design company called C. William Moss Associates, simply because I did not have a dime to my name and desperately needed a job. I had absolutely no bookkeeping skills and had never been a receptionist before (whatever that title even meant), but I had my father's big "I can do this" attitude. The company's founder and resident Renaissance man was a designer named Bill Moss who'd invented the Pop Tent, the very first "dome" camping tent. It was easy to put up and take down using lightweight fiberglass poles, and this pop-up tent completely revolutionized the camping market.

It was also the tent that turned my whole life upside down.

Chapter Nine

The Whole Place Was Odd

For my job interview at the Moss studio, I was told to take the driveway off Geddes Road in Ann Arbor, which was nothing but dirt, then to drive all the way through the woods to the end. The road crossed over a small bridge and curved past a few scattered buildings that looked like log cabins, but as I looked closer, I could see that the "logs" were made of concrete. I had never seen playful architecture like this before. In the middle of a nearby field was a concrete bowl fifty feet in diameter with sides that sloped to a large basin filled with water. A swimming pool? What was this place?

I followed the driveway to the end as instructed, and unlike all the other buildings in the compound, the studio was made of actual wood. It sat on a concrete slab, a long, narrow structure with a room on each side and walls that sloped out as they reached the roof. It reminded me of corn bins from my childhood on the farm. I parked and got out of my car, and just then, the front door of the studio flew open. A tall, thin woman hurried out, dressed in a white tailored shirt and khaki Bermuda shorts, with a tiny dog that followed behind her. "Who the fuck are *you*?" she yelled at me.

Before I could answer, she turned and hurled the cup she'd been carrying back through the open door. It shattered when it hit the inside wall. Then she shoved me aside, saying, "Get the hell out of my way."

With precision, she swooped down and picked up the miniature white poodle with one arm, shoved the dog into the large red leather bag hanging from her shoulder, and opened the door to a white Thunderbird convertible parked nearby.

The car spun out of the parking area, kicking up dirt and dust. For a few seconds, I didn't move. *What in the world was I getting myself into?*

I walked inside and closed the door behind me. I was standing in the reception room, where the soft, muted sound of a trumpet wafted from a room on the left. I turned to look through the open doorway.

The space was about twenty square feet, with large windows on three sides and views of Huron River. A white Formica counter rimmed the two walls under the windowsills, heaped with messy piles of documents and drawings, plus magazines, photos, pieces of fabric, and dirty plates and cups. A green upholstered barber chair stood in front of an old wooden drafting table, facing the river. A thin man with large black-framed glasses leaned back in the chair.

His graying hair protruded out in all directions, and he was wearing what I'd later come to think of as his uniform—faded blue jeans and a blue denim shirt with the sleeves rolled up to his elbows. He held a trumpet to his lips, and his long, thin fingers raised and lowered the valves. He used his other hand to stuff a handkerchief into the flared bell of the instrument to muffle some of the sound.

He stopped playing and swung the chair to face me, then wiped his mouth with the white handkerchief and looked at me over his glasses. Leaning forward, he put the horn on his drawing board and picked up a pipe. Still without speaking, he rubbed the bowl of the pipe against either side of his large nose, lit his Bic lighter, and directed the flame into the pipe bowl. He sucked and puffed until smoke filled the air around his face. Only after he'd finally put the lighter down on the drawing table did he speak: "Don't just stand there like an idiot. Get in here."

I walked into the room.

Was I scared? No. I had been raised on the farm to be fearless. And now my *modus operandi* kicked in: *You can do it. Just pretend you know what you're doing.*

"I'm here for an interview with Mr. Moss," I said. "My name is Marilyn."

Evidently, his pipe had gone out because he reached again for the lighter. At the same time, he motioned for me to sit beside his drawing board in a white plastic chair I later learned was a famous Saarinen "Tulip" chair.

"Oh yeah," he said. "I'm Bill Moss."

He sucked on the stem of the pipe for a few seconds and again tipped the Bic flame into the blackened bowl. Finally satisfied, he sat back in the barber chair, crossed his legs, and looked down at me until I started to feel uncomfortable and cleared my throat.

"That was nice trumpet playing," I said. "Peggy Lee's 'Cry Me a River'?"

"It isn't a trumpet. It's a flugelhorn."

"Oh? What's the difference?"

"A little flatter. Sounds are softer, more mellow." Smoke puffed out of his mouth with his answer. "Do you know Miles Davis's *Sketches of Spain?* Or Joe Bishop with Woody Herman? Or Chet Baker?"

I shook my head.

"They all play a flugelhorn. You got a lot to learn." He paused. "I see that you've already met Traci and her dog, Jazzy. Traci's temperamental. She's my business partner and a damn good artist, but she gets out of hand. Let's go have lunch."

"Don't you want to see my résumé?" I fumbled in my pocketbook to pull out the single, typed page.

Bill painting in his Michigan studio in the 1950s.

"No. I heard you type, keep books, and have some art background. That's fine. You can start tomorrow."

He took my elbow and ushered me to his car. Another convertible, this time, a Ford Fairlane. Black with a white leather interior. After opening the door for me, he got in, punched on the radio, then turned and smiled. "You're going to be perfect."

A few minutes later, we parked in front of what looked like a high-end restaurant, got out, and went inside. It was just what I expected: white tablecloths, leather booths, and waiters in full regalia. I had never been anywhere as fancy before.

"Good afternoon, Mr. Moss," one of the waiters said as we walked in, bowing ever so slightly.

"We'll have two Beefeater martinis, straight up, with olives," Bill told him, then walked straight to an empty booth.

Lunch was mostly a blur. I'd never had a martini before. He amused me with funny stories and ordered a second drink for each of us. I don't remember eating. As we drove back to the studio, I pointed to the buildings made of concrete logs. "What are those?"

"This entire complex was the Bennett Estate. Harry Bennett."

"Who's zat?" I asked, slurring my words.

"Harry Bennett. Henry Ford's bodyguard. You haven't heard of him?"

Bill didn't wait for me to answer.

"Bennett was a real thug. Always carried a pistol under his coat and had a shotgun leaning against his desk. Henry Ford hired him as a union buster, and Bennett acquired many enemies. He traveled with two large lions for protection."

I raised my eyebrows. "Live lions?"

"Yes, live ones. They sat on either side of his desk. He bought this land as a getaway and hideout, posted guards with machine guns at the road entrance. Booby traps everywhere."

Bill was still talking when we arrived back at the studio. We got out of the car and went inside. By now, I was unsteady on my feet. He lit his pipe again, then walked over to a corner of the room. I followed.

"See this chair?" he said. "Pick it up."

It was surprisingly easy to lift.

"Damn light, huh? These were the aluminum chairs used in the Ford Trimotor planes that used to fly passengers to the islands in the Great Lakes."

I sat down in it, slightly dizzy. "It's a beautiful shape—and comfortable." The ground was beginning to move under my feet. "What time do I come to work tomorrow?"

"Oh, nine or ten. I work late into the night. Before you go, let me show you the workshop."

A door led out of the office into a room of about fifty by fifty feet, with a concrete floor and high ceilings and an oversize garage door to the outside. The walls were lined with rolls of fabric and colored paper from floor to ceiling. A large, old, industrial Singer sewing machine made of glistening black cast iron sat in the middle of the floor, while several smaller versions lined one wall. Every other inch of space in that studio was claimed. There was a band saw, a standing drill, one long, highly varnished drawing table, several workbenches, and all kinds of different hand tools hanging on the walls. Charcoal and pen sketches had been tacked up helter-skelter everywhere there was space to hang them. Many, many small design models made of fabric or paper or foam board lay among dozens of glass jars of buttons and plastic parts and nails. I loved the richness of it all. I had never seen anything like it. So much creativity filled that room. So many unrealized ideas. A child's paradise.

I imagined sitting on a stool in there and simply *making things*. It was something I craved. I wanted to do it, every day. And it was something I felt so far away from in my own life. But in that studio, I knew I could build things, not unlike the fairy houses and forts I used to make at the farm out of sticks and rocks and moss. I could get messy again.

"See you in the morning," Bill said and turned away.

I drove down the driveway carefully, thinking, *Why didn't I ask more specifics about what I'll be doing here? And who will train me?* And then, *Are Bill and Traci lovers?*

The whole place was odd, but I couldn't lie. I liked it.

Chapter Ten
You Must Be a Little Crazy

Initially, I was Bill and Traci's jill of all trades. I worked part time typing letters (using a lot of Wite-Out), paying bills, and entering checks in the journal for the accountant. I took home a small check, earning $1.35 per hour, slightly more than minimum wage. The bookkeeping wasn't hard. Developing a sense of cash-in, cash-out didn't take long. There was always more going out than coming in, but the whole operation hummed with creativity.

Bill and Traci wandered in whenever it moved them. Work usually didn't start until late morning and sometimes went into the early hours of the following day. Deadlines were only met with the help of late-night surges and lots of coffee. It was like nothing I'd ever experienced, and I felt like *this* was the missing creative part of me. This was the life I wanted. This bohemian, chaotic, studio life. The makers' life. Adapting on the fly and making things up as we went.

It didn't take me long to get into the middle of Bill's crazy design work. He mentored me each day until I was able to help make some of the graphics and the layouts. New tasks were added to my work schedule almost daily. Sometimes I even modeled for the promotional photographs. But I worked mostly in the front office, struggling to cover company bills with half the required money.

Bill often drew at a drafting table in his big office with the door open, which allowed me to call out to him about each account.

Which one was the most important? Which one would he need to use again soon? Which one was a friendly supplier?

One day, there was a yell from outside. It sounded like "Help! Help! Help!"

"Bill! Who's that?" I said, racing to the window.

Bill answered without looking up. "Oh, that's just Sadie, the peacock. I used to have two, Sadie and Sally. One of my clients couldn't pay off his invoice, so he gave them to me instead. But Sally's gone now. She got run over by a UPS truck. He was a new driver and didn't see her admiring herself by the back wheel."

I rushed outside to get acquainted with Sadie, the beautiful and headstrong resident peacock. When I came back in, Bill was knocking the ashes out of his pipe into the wastebasket by hitting it on the sole of his shoe.

"Sit down," he said, "and I'll tell you a true story about someone who needed help."

It happened one night around two. He and Traci and a young man named Jay, who'd studied under architect Buckminster Fuller at the University of Michigan, were working to meet a deadline for a presentation on a line of animal toys made of a new lightweight material that Bill was obsessed with called foamcore. The toys were packaged flat, but they unfolded into three-dimensional shapes with holes in the center so that a young child could step into the hole and position the "animal" on their shoulders with straps: Hector Horse, Miss Mouse, Billy Bird, and Rusty Rooster.

Suddenly, a shriek sliced through the quiet of the studio: "Help! I can't swim!"

Bill and Jay hurried outside with a flashlight and scanned the river. Bill saw a man's head shoulder-deep in the water and shouted for him not to go any further. Then he pushed his rowboat into the water. When he reached him, the man started to climb in the boat, but Bill said, "Don't—it'll capsize. Grab hold of the stern, and I'll row you to shore."

Bill had started to think there was something strange about the guy. What was he doing in the river at two in the morning? But he brought him inside nonetheless, and Traci wrapped him in a blanket and made him a cup of coffee. She called emergency services while Bill was out in the boat. She reached the state police, where an officer said something to the effect of "That must be Eddie." They'd been looking for him after he'd recently escaped from the Ypsilanti State Hospital. Apparently, he thought he was Jesus and could walk on water. His story was later published in a well-known psychiatric case study on paranoid schizophrenia. But, on this night, Eddie sat in a chair in Bill's studio, looking slowly around the room as he sipped coffee. He motioned to one of Bill's new animal toys hanging from the ceiling. "You make that big bird?"

"Yes," Bill said.

"You make that big mouse?"

"Yes."

"And that yellow horse?" Eddie's eyes were growing wider.

"Yes, I did," Bill said. "Do you like them?"

"Uh-huh." Eddie rubbed his chin. Then he stared at Bill again and said, "You must be a little crazy."

Chapter Eleven

Each of Us Acting Our Parts

In the beginning, Bill Moss epitomized my idea of the creative rogue. He was charming, unpredictable, entertaining, unscheduled, funny, and self-centered. I liked so much about how he lived and how he thought about art and its connection to the everyday lives we all led. Moss wasn't making rarefied, precious art; instead, he was inspired by rule-breaking, innovative ideas, all in an effort to break down the stereotypes regarding what even constituted "art."

The ethos of the studio really suited me and provided an outlet for all the anger I felt toward the "establishment" back then. I was completely done playing by the rules and putting on fake costumes and trying to be perfect. The day I showed up for my interview at the studio was the beginning of my own transformative, creative journey. Because down deep, I was a maker—hungry to learn anything and everything creative.

Traci left soon after I started at the studio. Bill and I became lovers not long after that. I was twenty. Bill was nearly twice my age and sexy, charming, artistic, bohemian, and worldly. He was also great at romantic seduction. A drive up the Michigan peninsula in his convertible on a warm summer day. Picnicking on the sand dunes with wine, fruit, cheese, smoked sablefish, and a baguette.

Staying in a beautiful cabin on the lake. How was I, a young, easily impressionable woman, to resist?

Bill and his wife, June, had divorced before he and I met. She'd left for Aspen, Colorado, with their two sons, for whom Bill was, at best, an on-again, off-again father. I chose not to see the warning signs. It wasn't long after we met that I moved into Bill's house. I don't remember any discussions about me moving in. I don't remember him asking me. I don't remember thinking it over or even considering the idea. One day just melted into the next, and everything fell into place.

The glamour and fast-paced art world of Ann Arbor back then all made for a slightly crazed atmosphere. Bill's constant flow of design ideas, along with the never-ending parade of artists and celebrities who came to the studio, made it almost impossible to check in with myself. It was head-spinning for a good while—Ann Arbor at the height of its arts explosion. I honestly didn't know when I was being "myself" anymore and when I was pretending to be someone more worldly and refined.

Once again, the lines had blurred for me, and very quickly at that. Who was this latest version of Marilyn? Was I happy? I had no idea, and I didn't even have time to wonder. I was acting again, playing a different role than I'd played with Mom and Beac. Now, I was trying to please a very different person, named Bill.

The sixties in Ann Arbor was a wild time for a fresh-faced, impressionable, former Appalachian tomboy. The Vietnam War was exploding and imploding the political landscape, and I often found myself on the University of Michigan's Diag—a large, open diagonal space in the middle of Central Campus—protesting the war along with hundreds of other students. I campaigned vigorously for many progressive candidates back then, both locally and nationally, and I cheered John F. Kennedy when he gave his big speech on the Michigan Union stairs, introducing the Peace Corps.

During weekends, artists, musicians, and writers from Ann Arbor would all gather around the large fireplace at our house, discussing the war and the government and equal rights, although it soon became clear to me that Bill didn't really seem to care about any of it. He was a true designer in his mind—an "artist." He didn't deign to deal with such things as politics, and this was the first time I really saw him in a different, unsavory light. But there was no time to second-guess myself about him. No time to think at all, really. I was just out of college and young and naive enough to have gotten myself completely wrapped up in this new art world.

I had reinvented myself again and was right where I wanted to be—in a countercultural, rule-bending swirl filled with many different characters, all of whom paraded in and out of our kitchen, sleeping on any floor or couch or bed they could find and eating any food I could make them. I felt completely at home in the electricity and chaos of it all.

There was an art collective in Ann Arbor back then called the ONCE Group, a collection of musicians, visual artists, architects, and filmmakers at the forefront of the Ann Arbor scene. Around this time, John Cage, the iconic avant-garde composer, came to town to perform a new piece for them. His lodging for his Ann Arbor stay was none other than our guest room.

The night of his performance, John hit the strings of a grand piano onstage again and again with many different objects. It was a far cry from my uncles' banjo playing back in Elgood, but I was enthralled. The next day, John, who was an avid mycologist, and his friend, artist Robert Rauschenberg—everyone called him Bob—went on a wild mushroom hunt in the Michigan woods and returned to our house with a profusion of different varieties. I watched as they emptied several paper bags onto my kitchen counter, creating a massive mound of gorgeous fungi. While Bob rummaged through our cupboards, looking for soufflé dishes, John announced that he and Bob would make dinner. Oh, and by the way, he said, he'd invited the entire ONCE Group over too, along with lots of other out-of-town performers and friends.

"How many people, John?" I asked, alarmed.

"Sorry, Marilyn, I really don't know. First come, first served. I'd like you to make a couple of vegetable dishes and a large green salad. And, if there's time, can you make a really sweet dessert?"

I don't know how I pulled it off. Or why I had not yet begun to learn how to say no to demanding men like John. But cooking was in my DNA, and I'd been raised to pull off evenings like this. And just like Mom Nash, I liked nothing more than a crowd of people sitting around my table eating my food.

Between thirty and forty people came that night. John and Bob's soufflés kept appearing, one after another, until the pile of mushrooms dwindled, then disappeared. Not long after, a few of the guests became ill and were rushed to the emergency room. I wasn't one of them, thank goodness. I'd been too busy playing host and making salad to eat any of the soufflés.

Engrossed in this new life? Yes.

Enamored? Yes again.

Overwhelmed? Exhausted? Those, too.

There was so much newness flooding my life back then that it was all a blur and all incredibly exciting at the age of twenty-three. I certainly didn't have the aptitude at that young age to intellectualize any of it—I was just *in* it. Protesting the war and learning as I went at the Moss studio. There was no time to wonder if I was in the right place or in the right relationship. Bill and I became part of a play, each of us acting our parts. I was so caught up in the moment and in the energy of it all that I thought I was in love. But was I? I don't think so.

I wouldn't discover what real love was for many years to come.

Chapter Twelve

A Sign of What Was to Come

Bill and I got married in 1962 on an overnight business trip to Chicago, mostly just to help my mother feel better about the fact that he and I were "cohabitating." Looking back, I think the role of wife was just another part for me to play at that time, not one I'd given any real thought to whatsoever or had been planning on. It just "happened," like so many other things in my life back then.

On our first night of real matrimony, we were in our hotel room in Chicago after too many martinis, and we had our first true argument. It turned bad fast. I don't even remember what it was about, but I certainly remember that at one point, Bill slapped me hard—so hard that I fell to the floor.

He rushed to my side afterwards and begged my forgiveness, saying ". . . too much to drink . . . didn't know what I was doing . . . I'll never do it again—I promise."

We went to bed then, and I lay there wondering what had just happened to me. What I specifically thought was, what had *I* done to deserve it? With all the arguments that my parents had had, there had never been any violence, so I felt like it must have been *my fault* that Bill hit me. The well-trained people-pleaser in me reasoned that I had done something wrong—drank too much, maybe? Provoked him?

I promised myself that I would never drink like that again, and I kept that promise.

But Bill kept drinking—and fighting—with me.

He'd grown up in an abusive household and told me once that his father had "beat the crap" out of him. He often talked lovingly of his mother, who had died when he was a young child. His father didn't wait long before marrying a woman whom Bill described as "a true evil stepmother." She actively ignored Bill and sent him to school each day without any lunch, where he struggled because of his learning differences, drawing elaborate pictures at his desk instead of doing his assignments. Then his teacher would hit his hands with a wooden ruler and make him stand in the closet.

There was no sympathy at home from his stepmother. He felt entirely unseen and unloved. He once described to me the day he came home from school and found the house empty. "I took a kitchen knife and slit all of my stepmother's dresses in the closet into threads. Dad came home, saw what I had done, and said, 'Let's get the hell out of here.' We made a run for it."

Not long after we were married, Bill and I argued again. We'd just moved into Bill's house on Beechwood Street in Ann Arbor, and he'd come home drunk. He became angry when I asked him where he had been.

This time, I was ready.

When he tried to slap me, I was able to dodge his hand. Then I punched him so hard in his stomach that he fell back into the open closet. I took a breath and said, simply and firmly, "Don't you *ever* hit me again."

And he never did.

Because we were married and lived in his house, Bill obtained custody of his boys for a couple of months in the summer. During their first visit, I learned something very revealing about Bill, which I should have taken as a warning sign. Bill treasured his naps to the point where if anyone or anything woke him, he'd go into a rage. If his boys ever accidentally woke him up while roughhousing, Bill's bedroom door would fly open, and he'd run down the hall, yelling and screaming at them. One day that summer, David, the eldest boy, showed me a drawing he'd made. It showed a long hallway and a striped rug, with a well-drawn monster emerging from the door at the end. I recognized the setting instantly. It was our hallway rug and the door to our bedroom.

Chapter Thirteen

This Is Art, This Is Art, This Is Art

I f my marriage to Bill was built on the foundation of art and innovation and rule-breaking, it was also built on unhealthy compromise and a great deal of enabling on my part. Bill's infidelities started at the very beginning of our marriage.

The first time I discovered this fact, our son Jeff was only a year old. My stepfather Beac was staying at our house while attending a conference, and after I'd fixed dinner, Bill announced we'd been invited to a party at a friend's house. I didn't want to go and urged him not to. It was snowing, and the roads were slippery, but he went anyway.

When I woke up, it was three in the morning, and I realized he hadn't come home. Cell phones didn't exist then. I called the friend who'd hosted the party but got no answer. I checked on Jeff, who was sleeping soundly, and then woke Beac to let him know I was leaving to find Bill, convinced he must have gone off the road and was lying somewhere, unconscious.

The snow was still building up on the back roads as I crept along slowly, looking from side to side wherever the road had a ditch. There was no sign of our car. When I finally made it to the party, it was still in full swing. I walked around the cars parked at all angles in the field until I spotted our black Corvair between several cars and trucks. The windows were too frosted to see in, so I opened the door.

I saw Bill and a young woman, entangled in the backseat!

I slammed the door as fast as I could and hurried back to the car. The cold air froze the tears on my checks, and my lashes stuck together.

I woke up the next morning with Bill snoring on the other side of the bed. I lay there for a while, looking at him. Who was this person? What was I doing there? I felt sickened.

Then I found myself doubting what I'd surely seen in our car. Maybe he'd just passed out alone in that backseat? Maybe it was another couple who'd found our car unlocked and climbed in the back? Maybe I'd dreamt the whole thing? It was the start of a phase in which I really began to question myself. Was Bill really betraying me like this, seemingly without even trying to hide it? Was this really the state of my marriage? What had I done to deserve this? What was I not doing well enough? How could I get better?

I had a young son and no real money of my own. I was in over my head and didn't see a clear path out except forward, with Bill. I showed my contempt for him by staying aloof for days after I'd found him in the back of our car, but it didn't seem to bother him—or change his behavior at all. I considered leaving him again and again, but where would I go? We had the business together.

I would think about Jeff and the life he'd have without a father, and I would remember the real trauma I'd felt when my father left us. I decided that I would simply have to get stronger now—both in my own personal life and in the marriage.

This new resolve of mine gave me courage to stay. I was too busy to dwell on the pain of his betrayals. Or at least, that's what I told myself. I'd become very good at acting by now. I'd already shed "li'l MarilynRae" to become "Marilyn." I could put on any facade.

I quickly learned to fake my way through almost anything at the Moss studio. This skill came in handy whenever another public figure was drawn to Bill's designs and dropped by. It was an eclectic mix that included folks like Warren Avis, founder of the car rental company; Mary McFadden, fashion designer and writer; Patrick Lannan, director of the manufacturing company ITT Inc. and arts patron; and Henry Ford II, the car manufacturer. But as time wore on and I started to take on more responsibilities, I discovered how difficult it was to keep Bill focused. He started relying on me more and more, forcing me into a constant balancing act with his clients and contracts.

Now, he was bringing more of his clients to our house for dinner, where I had emerged as the company's gourmet cook, as well as secretary and bookkeeper and chief baby-bottle washer. I regularly repeated my trick of pretending I knew what I didn't and then doing what I didn't know how to do. Over and over, I told myself, *you can do this.* Fake it 'til you make it. But it was not a satisfying feeling in the end—to constantly pretend. And the more I did, the more Bill became the mad genius-child and I his reliable enabler.

In 1966, we sold the Beechwood Drive house and rented another house outside Ann Arbor in the nearby town of Ypsilanti, where we were once asked to house Andy Warhol and The Velvet Underground. They'd come to town to perform at a multimedia event called *Exploding Plastic Inevitable*, and, of course, we said yes. I may have been in a dysfunctional marriage; I may have been torn between staying or going; but I wasn't going to say no to the chance to meet Warhol and The Velvet Underground.

Warhol's colorful, beat-up van pulled into our driveway late at night, and eleven people crawled out. No problem identifying Andy: the jagged white wig, the round thick glasses, the phlegmatic look and constant composure. We only had two bedrooms in the rental house, so many of his crew slept on our couches or on throw pillows on the floor, or they used our camping mats. Many purple, orange, pink, and white heads were scattered throughout the house that night.

Early the next morning, our one-year-old son, Jeff, climbed out of his crib and began wandering the house. I can still see him in my mind, stopping at each colorful heap on the floor, then squatting down to take a better look. No one stirred at first. When the forms finally started to rise, I made bacon, scrambled eggs, and toast for hours as one zombie after another appeared in the kitchen. It was difficult to have much of a conversation with any of them. No one offered to help clean up.

As for Andy, he barely answered questions with a yes or no. He'd brought a film to the Ann Arbor Film Festival, *The Sleep*, which consisted of a man sleeping for six hours. My viewing only lasted three. That next morning, I asked Andy if he could tell me about it.

His reply: "A man sleeping."

There was no change in his stony, deadpan face. But I couldn't suppress a smile.

Our neighbor, a local farmer, called on the phone then and started yelling something about "no respect for people trying to make a living . . . no respect for private property . . . no respect for common decency."

It took me a few minutes to calm him down.

He told me that he'd recently plowed and tilled his fields for planting corn, but that morning, he'd gotten up at dawn only to discover the eerie sight of arms and legs sticking up out of the ground in rows. He was alarmed at first; then he took a closer look. They were mannequin parts. He said, "I knew instantly that someone at the hippie Moss house was the culprit."

He was correct, of course. Late the night before, Andy and his group had been out shooting a new film on the field entitled *Nico: Evening of Light* that featured the striking singer and model who'd attached herself to Warhol's group in New York and come to Ann Arbor.

What was I doing in the midst of all this? Even though I'd lived under the watchful eye and exacting rules of Mom and Beac for so many years, my life now ran counter to almost everything they'd tried to imprint on me. In this new world, manners and respectability had no currency. Yet it still it felt like a natural place for me.

That same fall, George Manupelli, an artist and filmmaker and professor at the University of Michigan, talked me into being in one of his films. A bit part, he said. No script. No sound. All I had to do was talk on the wall phone. I hesitated. George kept trying to convince me: "You just stand there, walk around a bit, and pretend to talk into the phone. Nude."

I wasn't sure I'd heard him correctly.

"Did you say *nude*? I have to stand with a phone in my hand without any *clothes* on?"

"That's right." He assured me that the film would be blurred and out of focus. "No one will recognize you."

Being an actor—at least, an "official" one—had never been one of my goals. But I said yes. I was so hungry for life back then. So hungry for experiences that I said yes to almost everything.

Still, being nude in front of a camera, even for a few minutes, was truly distressing. I kept mentally repeating to myself, *This is art. This is art. This is art.* Now I was breaking another rule—just like climbing the highest tree at the farm in Elgood. Making it up as I went, which, in many ways, I'd been doing since I was born.

Chapter Fourteen

Will Someone Find My *Poulet*?

I may have been an enabler, but I was also a survivor, and I was not going to give up on my marriage just yet. At one of the next anti–Vietnam War protests, I was one of many people arrested at the Diag on campus and taken to the police station and fingerprinted by the FBI. We got released, but the thought of going to jail frightened me, because by then, I was pregnant with our daughter, Genevieve.

I went home from jail to make bread. I'd found cooking was the thing that helped me to ground myself now. It took me back to the past and to Mom Nash's Sunday feasts and to Daddy's strong little MarilynRae. I think I also threw myself into cooking in Ann Arbor to protect my heart and to carve out my own territory in the marriage, separate from my domineering husband.

I had a friend in town named Pat Korten who taught me that everyday cooking could be like an art. She made the very best French baguettes I'd ever tasted, and I didn't know how to match them. One day, I asked her to share her secret; I figured the worst she could say was "no." Pat told me to get Julia Child's *Mastering the Art of French Cooking*. Then she said, "I have a better idea. Julia is a friend of mine—I learned directly from her. Maybe it's better if you learn from her, too."

I was stunned. Before I could answer, Pat picked up the phone, called Julia, and signed me up for her next cooking class in Cambridge, Massachusetts.

"Are you nuts, Pat? I can't afford a plane trip to Cambridge, let alone cooking lessons."

"Don't be silly. Of course you can. Find an inexpensive plane ticket—or drive. I'll talk to Julia about getting you a discount. If you want to make authentic French bread, you'll find a way."

And I did.

I left our young son in my mother's care—she and Beac were living in Grosse Pointe, Michigan, at this time—and drove the twelve hours to Cambridge in our old van. I didn't have any money for a hotel. Bill had outfitted the van with a padded rug, a long couch that extended into a bed for two, a camp stove, a sink, and a small fold-down table. Pat had wanted to call Julia and ask her if I could park the van in her driveway, but I'd said "Absolutely not, Pat. That's embarrassing. I don't want to overstep." But, as I drove around and around Cambridge, looking for a shopping mall parking lot to park in for the night, I wished I'd let Pat make that phone call. At last, I found a small lot and parked the van. I pulled the curtains closed, heated up some canned soup, and went to bed.

In the morning, I parked on tiny Irving Street in front of Julia Child's charming wooden house with all its flowers, shrubs, and trees, encircled by a picket fence. Three other women waited at the front door with me. Julia herself came to let us in, towering above all four of us.

I couldn't believe I was there. By what right? Mom Nash's face came to my mind then, along with her words: "You can be anything you want to be, MarilynRae."

Julia was warm and inviting, immediately breaking the ice by calling us by our first names. We followed her through her small sitting room filled with books and paintings into her cozy kitchen, no more than fifteen by fifteen feet—smaller, even, than my grandmother's kitchen in West Virginia. I stood near her open-hearth fireplace staring at Julia's bouquets of cooking spoons and spatulas in vases on the counter. She motioned for us to sit on the four wooden stools on one side of the table. "Wine?"

That first day, she served us a delicious Burgundy, and as we sipped, we frantically took notes while she demonstrated techniques for grating, chopping, slicing, dicing, whisking, beating, folding, grinding, puréeing, caramelizing, searing, and a great deal more. All of which she did easily. Effortlessly.

I remember how I shuddered when Julia whacked a large Vidalia onion with an enormous chef's knife, then diced it, the sound reverberating like a semiautomatic gun.

"Use *only* Sabatier knives," she told us, swinging the eleven-inch blade in a circle above her head. Her familiar singsong, high-pitched voice rang out as she chopped. "Sabatiers have the correct balance because they're made of carbon steel that runs through the handle, and they are the *only* ones to get a truly sharp edge."

Then she produced a whole plucked chicken, took another sip from her glass, set the glass down, and announced, "Now, don't be shy . . . just hack through the breastbone."

Nobody could cut up a chicken like Julia Child. But as she attacked the bird, it went flying off the cutting board and onto the floor.

"Oh dear," she laughed. "Will someone please find my *poulet*?"

A woman named Mary retrieved the poor bird and returned it to Julia, who placed it back on the cutting board, took another sip of wine, and said, "Now, where were we . . . oh yes, cutting through the breastbone."

"Aren't you going to rinse off the chicken?" Mary asked.

"Good heavens, no," Julia said. "The floor is clean."

We drank a lot of wine that day.

The next day, she served us Cabernet Sauvignon and promised to teach us to make French baguettes. Finally—the great secret!

The real reason I had come. I expected the revelation of some little, special ingredient. But flour, water, salt, and yeast—I couldn't believe that was all I saw on her breadboard.

Julia dumped a sticky, wet glob of dough onto the board from her mixing bowl and started working with it. The dough stuck to her right hand in a stringy mess. She took a five-finger pinch of flour with her left hand and scattered it on the board. Then she lightly touched her sticky right hand on some of the loose flour that she'd piled over to one side, while her left hand picked up a large spatula and scooped up the glutinous lump. Now she pushed the dough into her right hand, raised it shoulder-high, and slammed it down onto the table. Why wasn't she reaching for more flour?

As if reading my mind, she said, "You must work the dough as wet as possible, with little flour. It's a messy business. Work with as little flour as possible." Aha! At last, *the* secret.

Eventually, the roundish mass of dough started to take shape and became smooth and lovely. I wanted to cradle it in my hands. But the rising of the dough took many hours.

I looked at my watch when the bread finally came out of the oven. Making these three baguettes had taken all day. I had kids at home. An office to help run. Bills to pay. What was I doing? Still, it was the first time that I'd done something just for myself in years. The first time I'd followed my own heart in a long time. It felt so good. Each dish of Julia's had been made with passion and love, and I knew that I wanted to cook like that, too. Just like Mom Nash.

At the end of the last day, I was sad to leave, and as the other women stood in the kitchen thanking Julia, I went into the living room and sat down on her couch. I felt so comfortable there, so at home in the book-filled room. I imagined myself living in her house, cooking, and having dinner parties with a devoted husband. A man whom I could trust and who respected me as much as I did him.

I was startled out of my daydream by the women at the door, saying their good-byes. I jumped up from the couch and grabbed my purse and notebook from the kitchen. At the door, Julia gave me a big hug. "*Bon appétit.* Happy cooking!"

I returned to Ann Arbor and promptly got rid of our electric stove. I bought a large, secondhand commercial gas stove that I wasn't even sure would work because of all the mice that had made themselves comfortable in the ovens. But it did work. And every day, after teaching part-time at a nearby school and helping Bill at the studio, I would hurry home to my kitchen sanctum. These were the most joyful times of my week.

Soon Julia's French bread became a staple in our house, just like Mom Nash's biscuits at the farm.

Chapter Fifteen

What Good Mother Will Buy a Paper Sailboat for Her Kid?

I t was rare to see Bill anywhere without his pipe and a small black sketchbook. He carried both to meetings, to parties, and to bars and restaurants, no matter what the occasion. Cocktail napkins sometimes substituted for the sketchbook if they had to. Designs for toys, birdhouses, duck blinds, boats, ice-fishing shanties, beach sunshades, tents of all kinds, backyard or patio dining gazebos, a summer cottage, furniture—all took shape with the same elegant pen lines. All of these designs were to be constructed out of fabric or paper, folded into small packages, all embodying Bill's design philosophy: "Less is more." That was his mantra.

Our house was his testing ground, our rooms furnished with paper bookshelves, paper lamps, a paper couch, and two paper chairs with leather cushions, plus a paper doghouse for our English sheepdog, Samantha. One time, Bill went to New York City with a life-size paper sailboat that he'd carried into the office under his arm for a presentation at FAO Schwarz. Unfolded, the sailboat was big enough to carry two adults on the water, and several of us had recently sailed it on the Huron River. As the story goes, Bill now unfolded this paper catamaran in front of an enormous, mahogany desk in the buyer's office. The boat was made of foamcore and treated with a Teflon coating. Bill said proudly, "My wife and my ten-year-old son each sailed this alone on the Huron River."

The buyer took a big puff on his cigar, blew the smoke straight out, and said, "That's real cute, Mr. Moss, but what good mother is going to buy a paper boat for her kid to sail on the water?"

Bill didn't mind, because by now, he'd already moved on to other projects. He was constantly creating something new. His creative buzz was his real high—his reason for being.

Unfortunately, he was not the businessman he thought he was—or even a reliable product developer. He would often leave one investor stranded while finding a new one. Sometimes, he sold the same design to two different clients.

I didn't know what to do. This pattern was repeated over and over, for years: Bill would come up with a revolutionary design and get paid for the exclusive license. A retainer fee was usually doled out monthly for the development of the design, with an execution schedule included as part of the agreement. More often than not, Bill was either late or he'd never complete the project at all.

Once, Bill designed a brilliant tent called the Bubble Tent for the Ford Motor Company—a dome-shaped nylon tent in a metal tube that could be fastened on top of a Ford station wagon. You pulled the tent out from the rear of the station wagon, and it turned into a full, stand-up camping tent, providing a sleeping area for four or five. As usual, Bill attracted a lot of press with the project, and requests for the tent started pouring in. But also as usual, Bill lost interest in working out the production details, and the Bubble Tent never came to fruition.

Getting a design ready for production was not Bill's forte. Instead, with the help of a martini—or two, or three—at the local bar, he would create another new design on a cocktail napkin and set sail in a new direction. This would soon grow to infuriate me.

Chapter Sixteen

The Speedometer Read 120

In June of 1966, Bill came home after a design presentation in Detroit and said, "I hope your passport is up-to-date. We're going to France and Italy."

"I don't have a passport," I told him. "I've never traveled outside the States. And Bill, we are overdrawn at the bank. We owe rent, and we have other bills to pay. How can we afford to travel abroad?"

Bill wasn't concerned. He wasted no attention on small details like paying bills.

"You and I have been hired to travel with and photograph Carroll Shelby and the Ford Racing Team. We'll be in France, Italy, and Monte Carlo."

"Who's Carroll Shelby?" I asked. "And I didn't know Ford had a racing team."

"He was at the meeting this morning. Ray Geddes introduced me."

Ray was a good friend and an advisor to Bill, and he served as the treasurer on our board of directors.

"Carroll is a he?" I said.

"Carroll is a well-known race-car driver who designs and builds cars. And no worries—Ray said Ford is paying for everything on top of our fee."

Ray stopped by our design studio a few days later and told us that Shelby's goal was to enter his Cobra race car in the 24 Hours of Le Mans and beat all the Ferrari cars. The endurance-focused race is won by the car that covers the greatest distance over a twenty-four-hour period. As one of the top American race car drivers, Shelby had a long rivalry with Ferrari, but because of a heart condition, he had been forced to retire. "The Cobra is his baby," Ray told me. "He's quite a character. You two will have a blast."

Passport in hand—thanks to an expedited service—and the children secured with my mother and Beac, Bill and I headed to Paris hauling all kinds of heavy photography equipment.

Shelby's secretary had made hotel reservations for us, and when our taxi driver pulled up to the hotel's front door, I said, "Oh, *mon Dieu!*" and poked the driver's shoulder. I was struggling with my high school and college French, but I managed to say *Il y a sûrement une erreur* ("There must have been some mistake"). Rolls-Royces kept pulling up to the curb next to us outside of what appeared to be a castle.

Again, I showed the driver the paper with the hotel name and address.

"*Non, madame,*" he said in slow English. "There is only one George V."

I looked at the women and men emerging from the other cars, so stylishly dressed and smothered with gold and jewels. Both Bill and I were wearing blue jeans.

Bill just nodded. "Ray told me that Carroll travels in style. He's just trying to impress us."

"Well, he's succeeded."

A doorman opened the heavy brass and glass doors, and we walked inside. I became even more self-conscious. The lobby was huge, with a floor of intricately designed marble. A massive glass chandelier hung from the middle of the ceiling, above a round, ornately carved table. On the table was a fresh flower arrangement at least six feet high. Everyone, particularly the staff, stared at us. I tried a weak smile, but no one reciprocated. Our shabby, worn luggage and our photography gear stood out vividly against the stylish Louis Vuitton valises lined up at the concierge desk.

The dissonance increased when we were led to our room. Make that *rooms*. They were elegantly furnished to resemble a stately mansion: two bedrooms with large beds, a living room with an elaborate marble fireplace, a smaller sitting room, also with a fireplace. And yet another fireplace in a small library area filled with French books and newspapers. Bill poured himself a drink from the small, well-stocked bar, smiling from ear to ear, then sat down on one of the empire chairs in the library, crossed his legs, and lit his pipe.

I pointed to the large safe in the library. "And exactly what do we squirrel away in here—my silver bracelets and wedding band?" I never usually took off either.

"Our valuables, of course." Bill got up and reached into one of our bags. "Film and cameras."

The bathroom was equally grandiose, with huge gold mirrors, a marble floor and counters, and gold faucets. "Wow! Two toilets," I yelled. "Bill, come check this out."

"That's a bidet," he said, laughing.

"What's that?"

"You sit on it and wash your underparts."

"Oh, how civilized."

Le Mans sat about three hours southwest of Paris. The ancient city on the Sarthe River had been home to the famous race since 1923. We drove down there the next morning and could hear the roar of cars long before we arrived. We went straight to the track.

I unpacked my gear and knelt in the grass at the edge, propping my Rolleiflex camera on one knee. I had been doing the product photography for Moss now for a few years, but I never photographed anything so fast and dramatic as those race cars before. The continuous noise surged through my skull, and

Me, exhausted while waiting at 24 Hours of Le Mans, in 1966.

the acrid smell of fuel, rubber, and carbon monoxide seeped into my lungs. But I was determined to get some good shots. I leaned into the track with a telescopic lens as the cars came around the turn, trying to get shots of the powerful thrust of the cars. Then I retreated at the last moment before the racers reached me—a difficult maneuver—and during those terrifying split seconds, I was never quite sure what image I'd managed to capture.

After a few hours on the edge of the track, Bill and I climbed the stairs to Ford's viewing box, hoping for some respite from the noise and stench. The crowded box was filled with Ford dignitaries and more of the same type of glamorous women we'd seen at the George V, draped in silks and gold. It seemed that every man had a champagne bottle in one hand and a glass in the other. I elbowed my way to the railing and leaned over with my camera as the cars sped by, taking one shot after another. Finally, I pulled back and turned directly into a cloud of cigar smoke, behind which was Lee

Iacocca, vice president of Ford Motor Company. "And who are *you?*" Iacocca asked.

I wasn't sure how to answer.

Bill intervened. "Lee, this is my wife, Marilyn."

Lee backed off a little and reached to shake my hand. "Marilyn, how did you get hitched up with this character? It's a pleasure to meet you."

Over the next two days, I met many famous race car drivers, listened to the relentless noise, drank copious amounts of champagne, and took at least thirty rolls of pictures. Being there was thrilling, and I felt *important* with my press pass and cameras. But I didn't truly fit in. You could only take the Appalachian tomboy out of me to a degree. I didn't do glamour. I didn't do high fashion or jewels and wouldn't even if Bill and I had the money. Eventually, all that glamour turned into headaches and nausea. When the race was finally over and the Cobras and Shelby-American cars had won, I was eager to go to bed.

Instead, Carroll said, "Come on, you two chicken-grabbers. We're all gonna go out to celebrate. Dine and drink *real* fine."

I was too tired to remember what we ate, but I do know that the champagne continued to flow. Cognac and cigars were abundant, too. My eyes had begun to droop when one of the race car drivers, Dan Gurney, announced, "I'm going back to where we've been booked to sleep tonight. Does anyone want a ride?" Dan was the only person in the room who hadn't been drinking.

"Yes!" I shouted and grabbed Bill's arm to drag him out. We'd been awake for thirty-three hours straight. My life felt like a continuous movie but one in which I only had a supporting role and was not in any way in charge of directing.

When we arrived at what I assumed was our new hotel in Le Mans, there weren't any lights on in the building. Dan, who was clearly familiar with the place, led the way inside, and we followed him down a long corridor. He halted briefly and pointed to a door, saying, "Here's the bathroom." Then he opened another door and switched on a light. Inside was one large room. A dormitory? Barracks?

Fourteen single beds, seven on each side, stood closely lined up against both walls. A lamp sat on a small table between every two beds. Dan said, "Those two beds down at the end are yours." Not exactly the George V. That night, I was the only woman sleeping in a room with thirteen men. But still, I felt more at ease without all the opulence.

The next day, we were hustled off for the next race at Rouen, about a three-hour drive northeast of Le Mans. After that race, Bill and I, along with the entire Ford Racing Team, gathered to celebrate at a small, four-star restaurant in the French countryside. This time, many more guests showed up—at least thirty people in all—a gaggle of drivers, crew, managers, photographers, race car magazine writers, and newspaper reporters. And Bill and me. Carroll Shelby repeated his now all-too-familiar shout to a waiter, in a thunderous voice. "Hey, you chicken-grabbin' *gaaarsahn!* Get your tail over here and get these mighty fine people a drink!"

The noise level increased with each round. French diners at a couple of small tables near us looked at us with contempt, as if to say, "*Dégoûtant!* Ugly Americans." I was embarrassed and wanted to hide under the table.

Carroll ordered the best and oldest wines and cognacs up from the cellar. At the end of the meal, one waiter placed a glass snifter by each of our plates. Another waiter presented each of us with a Cuban cigar. He started with Carroll, waiting for the nod, then he came to me and rolled the end of the cigar slowly around the tip of the flame until the cigar was evenly lit. "Madame," he said, and handed it to me.

I stared at it. I had never held a cigar in my hand. But I watched Carroll, and after a few coughs, I found a comfortable puff level. Who knew that I'd like cigars or that it would mark the

Me driving Carroll Shelby's Cobra along the California coast in the 1960s. Photo by Bill Moss.

beginning of an occasional pleasure? But now it was time to go home—back to Ann Arbor and the children. Time to try to piece together our life.

I dreaded what I knew I'd face there: the debt and Bill's drinking, his infidelities piling up. This was not the creative life that I'd imagined. Not the marriage I wanted. Some part of myself had been tamped down by all the hustle to make our high-wire act work. Where was plucky MarilynRae? Where had she run off to? Trying to please Bill was exacting just as high a cost as trying to please my mother all those years. The price? My own sense of self. My autonomy. My resolve.

After we got back from France, I got a call from Carroll. "Marilyn," he said. "Hugh Hefner just bought a new Cobra from me. How'd you like to drive to Chicago and deliver that sweet little machine to him?"

"Just hand me the keys." Part of me was always ready for my next adventure, an escape hatch to get away from Bill and the destruction he left in his wake.

With my friend Marie along for company in the passenger seat, I drove Hugh Hefner's Cobra to Chicago. Somewhere in Indiana, a Corvette Stingray with two young men in it appeared on our left and started yelling at us, although I couldn't hear what they were saying. They crossed over to our lane, very close to our car, obviously trying to slow us down. But we had a deadline to meet.

I looked over at Marie and said, "Enough of this game. Hold on."

I downshifted and moved to the left to pass.

The Corvette sped up to match us.

I went a little faster.

So did the Corvette.

"Wave good-bye to them, Marie!" I yelled.

She did, and I floored it. There was a part of me that wanted to just keep driving and never look back. We left them in our exhaust. The speedometer read 120.

Chapter Seventeen

I Wasn't Going to Give Up

Bill's addiction to parties and people and action, always action, continued. In the summer of 1967, he and our then business partner, Paul, hatched a scheme: C. William Moss Associates, Inc. would host an unforgettable dinner to thank our Detroit clients and cultivate new ones. The meal would be highly unconventional for the Midwest—an authentic Maine lobster bake in our workshop's paper dome. Would I help them pull the whole thing off?

In 1953 my mother had bought a small, dilapidated fishing shack in a small cove on North Haven Island in Maine for five-hundred dollars after visiting friends there. It was the start of my long love affair with the state of Maine, one I have never outgrown. Lobster bakes on the beach had become a regular ritual in our lives there whenever I got to go. I knew about lobsters. And yes, I'd help Bill and Paul pull off a Maine lobster bake in Michigan. What I didn't know was that this zany party would end up stirring a keen desire in me to live year-round in Maine.

We mailed eighty invitations to Ford executives and their wives and to the various advertising agencies. The yeses poured in. Eventually, the tally grew to one hundred. When Paul and Bill told me how many people would be descending upon us, I stared in disbelief.

"Are you two crazy?" I asked, knowing the question was rhetorical. We were all aware of what Paul and Bill could pull off when they set their minds to it. Maine lobster was not easy to buy in Michigan, and it was very expensive and never truly fresh. Have no fear. From one of our contacts in Maine, Paul ordered 115 lobsters, plus dozens of clams and barrels of seaweed. All for overnight delivery on the morning of the gala, along with kegs of Löwenbräu. Then Paul and Bill and I moved all the sewing machines and machinery out of the main workshop and positioned several eight-foot plywood sheets, covered with white butcher paper, on wooden horses. We rented folding chairs, and Paul's wife Carolyn and I put a line of small round cast-iron pots for melted butter down the center of each table, with a lobster claw cracker, a fork, a knife, a plastic wineglass, and a stack of paper napkins in front of each plate.

We all worked together to remove the enormous plastic roof from the experimental paper dome. This was the kind of project I loved working on with Bill; it played to both our strengths, mixing my love of gathering people around food with his love of breaking all the rules on what a party could even be.

The day before the gala, Paul and Bill collected rocks from the woods near the studio, all four to six inches around, and placed them in a twenty-foot-diameter circle on the ground inside the dome. Later that night, we all piled branches and small logs on top of those rocks and started the fire. Paul and Bill took turns throughout the night to get the fire right and the rocks red hot. Then, in the morning, Carolyn and I peeled one hundred potatoes and one hundred onions and cut up seventeen chickens and five pounds of sausages and ten pounds of carrots. Then we shredded thirty cabbages for coleslaw and tore up a dozen heads of lettuce and diced dozens of tomatoes, cucumbers, and red and yellow peppers for the salad. UPS came through with the lobsters, clams, and seaweed.

Just hours before the dinner was to start, Bill and Paul scraped off the fire and piled the food on the hot rocks, just like I had done many times in Maine. A layer of seaweed. A layer of chicken pieces. Another thin layer of seaweed. Then the sausage links, potatoes, and onions. More seaweed. Then the lobsters. Then even more seaweed, and finally, the clams. After we were done, we stretched a heavy tarp over the enormous mound. The scene was set.

As they arrived, Paul handed each guest a shot glass of aquavit and a separate glass of freshly tapped Löwenbräu. He wouldn't let anyone enter the dome until they'd downed their shots and chasers. All the men arrived in suits or sport jackets and ties. The women were turned out in Chanel suits, pillbox hats, high heels, and nylon stockings. I felt incredibly underdressed in my jeans and black turtleneck (not that I owned any better outfits).

"We did put 'informal' on the invitations, didn't we?" I whispered to Paul.

"I don't think this group knows what informal means." Paul smiled.

As the party progressed, our guests went back for refills of aquavit and Löwenbräu. Ties and jackets were removed, high heels abandoned. Everyone seemed to be having a very good time though some eyed the smoldering heap in the dome with suspicion. Finally, Paul announced in a loud voice, "Come and get it. Maine lobster, now being served."

He pulled back the tarp, and the crowd gasped as the delectable aroma billowed forth. Our guests marched toward the steaming mound, many of them asking me, "Do you really do this on the shores in Maine?" We did, in fact. It crossed my mind then that if only Bill and I could move there permanently and leave all of this behind, maybe Maine could solve our problems.

Our peacock Sadie, who witnessed the event from the yard, didn't know what to make of it. And even though my marriage was very wobbly by then, this party helped level it for a while. Maybe it was because I felt more included in Bill's world that night— together, we'd pulled off something unique. Maybe it was all the aquavit and beer and wine we consumed afterward, cleaning up. But somehow, I felt connected to Bill again in a new way, and for a moment, it gave me hope for my marriage. Hope for our family. I wasn't going to give up on it yet.

Chapter Eighteen

Summers in Paper Domes

F ollowing that lobster bake in the paper dome, it seemed like everything in me wanted to move up to Maine. I longed for a life with animals again and had this idea that I could find some land and re-create part of my childhood farm.

In the summer of 1953, Mom and I had visited two teacher friends named Berta and Connie who had a cottage on North Haven Island in Penobscot Bay, fourteen miles off the shore of Rockland. After Mom had driven her car onto the ferry, I got out and watched in amazement as we maneuvered through all the boats in the harbor. An hour or so later, we entered the Fox Islands Thorofare. As it happened, I was standing on the ferry deck next to Charles Lindbergh's wife, Anne Lindbergh, who owned a summer home on North Haven. She must have realized I was a disoriented newcomer because she began pointing to landmarks: "This is North Haven. And on the right is Vinalhaven."

I could have never known how much I'd relish my first visit there. Walking into Berta and Connie's snug house was like walking into a little monastery. Safe, warm, peaceful, and calm. Connie's father had been a sea captain there, and the island was her longtime home. Life on North Haven reminded me of Elgood and the Nash farm—daily baking, sharing old Maine recipes, tending to Connie and Berta's storybook vegetable and flower gardens, and clamming on the mudflats—it all brought back the sharing and caring and love in our farmhouse. I hadn't realized how much I craved it.

Three days before Mom and I were scheduled to leave, Connie put down her fork at breakfast, dabbed her mouth with a cloth napkin, and said, "Lucille, I think you should buy a place here. Both you and Marilyn love it." Before Mom could manage to respond, Connie continued. "And I know a place for sale that you can afford."

She paused.

"It does need some work," she said, shaking her head from side to side. "Actually, a lot of work. But Berta and I can help you."

Mom looked at me. I was smiling and ready to explode.

That small fisherman's house that my mother ended up buying in Bartlett Harbor, North Haven Island, was in deplorable condition, and I'm not sure what gave her the courage. I know she didn't have much money. But together, we learned to steam off old wallpaper, remove old paint, and patch, putty, and sand the old, plastered walls. Mom hired a heating and plumbing man on the island named Rex, who checked out the chimney and fireplace and tested the water pumped in from a well and straightened up the outhouse. Each year, little by little, we upgraded. Then Beac started coming with us to North Haven, and a few years later, a much larger house with a big barn on the North Shore Road was listed for sale. Mom and Beac bought this old farmhouse on forty-some acres, with many feet of shoreline. By this time, I was married with two children of my own and I longed for a place on the island to call our own.

Bill and I didn't have any money to buy a house or land on the island, but for a while, he had been excited by these new, tapered, sixteen-foot-long, Upson foamcore panels. He'd also talked DuPont into treating the outside of these panels with a Teflon coating so he could try using them to build two domes for us on North Haven.

Our "paper" summer home on North Haven Island, installed in 1968. The domed walls are made of Teflon-coated foamcore panels and the doorways are fabric canopies.

Mom and Beac said yes, as long as the domes were down the hill, out of their sight. Mom warned, "Just don't block our view of Camden Hills."

That summer of 1968, Bill and I, along with a young artist from Ann Arbor, installed two attached Upson domes on the island—one was twenty-five feet in diameter, the other ten feet. We put them up on a fifty-by-fifty-foot-wide, thirty-foot-high wooden deck above the spruce treetops on the side of a hill descending to the shore. The year-round residents of North Haven Island were skeptical. The domes seemed like they were from a different planet. Rumors spread fast throughout the island about Lucille's daughter and her bohemian artist husband.

"Houses made of paper? Just plain crazy."

"The domes won't last through the first nor'easter. It'll take them right out to sea."

"They're artists from Michigan. They don't know any better."

A daily parade of islanders came by to check out the domes. Most didn't say anything out loud, just shook their heads. The most curious were the younger artists who seemed truly fascinated.

Two large, sliding glass doors were inserted into the panels of the bigger dome that flanked a Franklin fireplace. These doors provided a spectacular panoramic view of Penobscot Bay sunsets and Camden Hills. Inside, my dome kitchen consisted of a large iron sink, a small propane four-burner stove and oven, a small gas refrigerator, a counter and shelves curved into the wall, and an old butcher's block. We had water pumped up from a stream. A compost toilet, which we used even in the rain while wearing ponchos, sat outside. During the day, the dome was full of light, even when it was cloudy outside. At night, gas lights, kerosene lamps, and candles provided cozy lighting. It was a good time for our little family. Bill stayed with us for weeks at a time and seemed calmer and less maniacal and moody.

But dome living on an island had its challenges. Getting from the domes to the island's only doctor at night with a sick or injured child was one of the biggest. Early one evening during our first summer in the domes, Bill was out on the water in our little boat, fishing with Jeff. As Bill cast his line out into the water, the hook lodged in Jeff's left earlobe. Fifteen minutes later, Bill and Jeff arrived back at the domes. Jeff was screaming. The lure dangled from his bloody ear like an earring. Bill said in an agitated voice, "I'm trying to get him to let me take it out, but he won't let me touch it."

Jeff screamed, "*No!* It'll hurt more!"

I put Jeff in the car and drove to my parents' house, relieved to see the downstairs lights on. I knew there was a doctor somewhere on the island, but I didn't know his name or where he lived. My mother did. We jumped in the car. The doctor was kind and patient and numbed Jeff's ear, then deftly removed the hook and lure. It was our only Jeff-related island calamity.

But Genevieve was another species. I had to watch over her carefully. She managed to break a leg when she was only six months old. Not one to let a full leg cast keep her down, she pulled herself along using a coffee table or chair and learned to walk by using the stiff, cast-enveloped leg to help her stand. By the age of one year, Genevieve was already fearless and ran everywhere as fast as her fat little legs could move, usually toward danger. Once at my parents' house for an overnight, she'd grabbed hold of the electrical cord attached to the coffeepot, pulled it off the table, and got third-degree burns on her shoulder. A year later, she fell over the back of the couch in the dome and landed on her head on the wooden floor. It knocked her out and sent her into a convulsion. Once again, I had a heart-stopping car ride from the domes to the doctor's house. He was able to stop the convulsion, and I thought the incident was over.

Except that it wasn't. For the next few months, every time Genevieve fell, which was often, she would again start to convulse. It took days of tests at the University of Michigan hospital to learn that in some cases involving head injuries like hers, a later fall, even a little one, would trigger a recurrence of the initial traumatic response. The doctor trained me on what to do each time Genevieve took a fall. I needed to get down on my knees, so my eyes were level with hers. Then I grabbed each of her shoulders firmly and, in a stern, loud voice, said, "Genie! You're all right. You're not hurt. Take a breath. Take a breath."

At first, this sounded crazy to me. The doctor was telling me to talk my daughter out of a convulsion? But I tried it, and it worked. The convulsions stopped. At the end of that summer, when friends asked me what I'd done on the island, I said, "Mostly, I tried to keep Genevieve alive."

Despite all that, living in those domes on the island in the summers was the place where our little family was happiest together. The domes not only outlasted their first nor'easter but would stand proudly for ten more harsh Maine winters. Living in them, I felt more like myself than I had during my whole marriage to Bill. I was back on the land, connecting to nature, contending with the weather like we'd done each day on the farm.

Chapter Nineteen

Here, Maybe I Could Put Down Roots

T hen, in the spring of 1970, we did it. We moved to Maine year-round. I drove our Ford van from Ann Arbor to Rockport, while Bill stayed in Ann Arbor to finish a few projects for the business. There was barely enough room in the van for the kids and all our stuff and our large English sheepdog, Samantha—taller than either of the children when she sat on the car seat. I'd learned to weave rugs under the tutelage of Peter Collingwood, a renowned British rug-maker and was bringing in additional income working on commissions. At first, we wondered how I could get my immense floor loom from Ann Arbor to Maine. In the end I rented a U-Haul trailer and hitched it to the back of the van.

After an eighteen-hour nonstop drive, Jeff, Genevieve, Samantha, and I arrived, and right away, I knew this was where we belonged—Rockport, Maine. Population 3,000. A small, coastal town with a deep harbor. Since Bill wouldn't come until later, I rented a small apartment in the center of town in an old, large wooden Victorian. But then I saw a "For Sale" sign on a house nearby—an old, rambling, two story with tiny rooms that had been divided into two rental units. The cost was $15,000. It needed lots of work, and we only had $1,200 in our bank account now, the dribs and drabs of royalties from Bill's few remaining licensed designs at this point.

I walked into the local bank in Camden and talked my way into a mortgage, plus a $20,000 fix-up loan. Then, right after the sale and the tenants had moved out, I began tearing down walls and painting and sanding like mad. A few days later, I was in the back of the house, covered in white dust, a plastering hawk tool in my left hand and a trowel in my right, when I heard the familiar voices of my loan officer, Ted, and his colleague, Dick, from the bank.

"Marilyn, oh Marilyn, where are you?" Dick yelled in a singsong voice.

"I'm back here!" I shouted. "Watch your step."

Ted and Dick stepped carefully through the front room, balancing like tightrope walkers on the planks that covered gaping holes in the floors. Plaster and Sheetrock dust were everywhere.

"My God, Marilyn," Ted exclaimed, staring down through one of the holes into the dirt-floor basement below. "There's not much left to the house, and your first mortgage payment isn't even due yet."

I put down my tools and did my best to brush off the dust that clung to my T-shirt and cut-off jeans.

"Welcome," I said. "Take a good look, because next time I give you a tour, it's going to look like something out of *House Beautiful*."

Ted glanced around the room and rubbed the back of his neck. "Dick and I thought we'd see what you were doing with the loan I gave you to fix up your house."

"Looks like instead of fixin' up, she's tearin' down," Dick said.

"Come on," I said. "Let me tell you my plans." I was exhilarated now. Not since my years at the farm had I felt so at home in any one place. Here, I could put down roots. Here, maybe I could take my costume off.

I led the men through the house, room by room. By the time we were finished, Ted looked a little stunned. He turned to me. "Did I really loan you enough money for all of that?"

The room at the top of the stairs became the master bedroom, and I instructed the painter to spray whitewash on the beams and ceiling—an idea I'd gotten from *Better Homes and Gardens*. There was a tiny bathroom off the bedroom with a rusted metal shower stall, a toilet, and a small sink. This would never do. But I had a plan. All the locals knew that the North Haven Island dump was a great place to find treasures discarded by summer people who redecorated their old cottages. Every few days, I went over to the island and visited the dump, patiently watching for the perfect item to appear. For several weeks, I had no luck. Then, one day—bingo! There was my treasure: a white-enameled, cast-iron, seven-foot-long, claw-foot bathtub. It glimmered in the sunlight and weighed a mere five hundred pounds.

For the next several weeks, the plumber and I tore that tiny upstairs bathroom of mine to pieces, then began the careful work of remodeling. Meanwhile, the tub sat on a small patch of grass at the front door of the house. Neighbors stopped to examine it, and children climbed in and out of it. Everyone who saw it asked me for an explanation.

"Why such a big one?"

"Why go to so much trouble and expense for this old monstrosity?"

"Why not get a new fancy blue or pink tub from Sears?"

My kids were embarrassed. One neighbor asked them, "Why does your mommy keep that tub outside?"

But finally, the bathroom was ready, and the day arrived to move the five-hundred-pound monster to its home. I convinced George and Andy, two carpenters working on the house, to use a dolly and a rope. With a lot of cursing about "Mrs. Moss's tub," the two got the bathtub through the front doorway and up the steep,

Genevieve, Samantha the English Sheepdog, and Jeff in Michigan in 1971.

narrow, rickety steps. The tub looked regal on a sunken, one-step, carpeted platform throne where it took up most of the seven-and-a-half-by-eight foot room. I veneered all the walls with mirrors to create the illusion of a much larger space, and a week later, Bill arrived from Ann Arbor. I was so proud of my restoration work when I gave him a tour. He was captivated with the bathtub.

Early the next morning, he filled it, and then he, Jeff, and Genie climbed in. I was downstairs in the kitchen making breakfast, listening to *Morning Edition* on Maine Public Radio. The tub was directly over the kitchen stove, and I could hear the kids laughing and splashing water. I was partially listening to the news report and partially daydreaming, thinking maybe we could really make this marriage work in Maine. Suddenly, I heard another sound—faint but distinctive.

I turned off the radio. At first, I thought I must have imagined it, but a few seconds later, I heard it again—a disturbing sound, like wood ripping. I looked up at the large, exposed wooden carrying beam above my head. The noise repeated itself. Then I saw it. The beam was splitting!

I took off running for the stairs. I ran past Andy, who was in my weaving room, Sheetrocking the walls, and I blurted out something about impending disaster, then hurried up the stairs two at a time, racing into the bathroom. Bill and the kids were still in the tub, laughing, and when I burst in, the kids turned and stared at me like startled kittens. I plunged my arm into the water and pulled out the rubber plug.

"Get out!" I shouted. "All of you! Now!"

"Why, Mommy?"

"Just do as I say. Grab some towels and get downstairs. Quickly!"

"What the hell's going on?" Bill yelled back.

"The beam is breaking!"

I ran back downstairs. Andy was pushing back his cap, scratching his head, and looking up at the approaching calamity. Andy never moved quickly. He and George pounded nails with the same rhythm they employed for walking and talking and chewing their lunches.

"Andy!" I yelled. "For God's sake, do something!"

He walked slowly and calmly out into the hall, then yelled upstairs to George, who was laying insulation in the attic: "George! Better get down here. Seems Mrs. Moss's tub is coming into the kitchen."

His request sounded like a weather report on a good day. I wanted to scream at him.

Then George ambled downstairs into the kitchen, past me, and down into the cellar. I started grabbing glassware off the shelves as fast as I could. My mind was filled with images of the tub falling, water splashing everywhere, glass splintering and ricocheting across the room, the counter splitting in half and the newly laid floor tiles breaking.

But in a slow-motion fog, I saw George reappear from the basement carrying an adjustable, metal floor jack. He set it down on the kitchen floor. With excruciating slowness, he and Andy raised it inch by inch, toward the beam.

Then I heard it—*whump!*

I looked at the beam in disbelief. It had split fully through. Its two end pieces sat neatly on the metal plate of the floor jack as if they'd belonged there all along. George and Andy had been able to set the floor jack under the beam right at the exact instant the beam had cracked completely.

Andy took off his cap and wiped his forehead with his handkerchief. George was still looking up and shaking his head. Bill ran into the kitchen with a towel wrapped around his waist, the kids right behind him. My heart thrashed about in my chest.

"Guess you tore out too many walls down here," Andy said.

For the next several weeks, the rumor flew around town: "Did you hear about Mrs. Moss's tub falling into her kitchen?"

Chapter Twenty

Space to be Happy

Even after that house renovation, I found myself driving around the roads outside Rockport, yearning for actual land. A space for a garden and animals. The smells and warmth of the Elgood farm were still stuck to my ribs. One day, I stopped in front of an old cape on Mill Street in West Rockport and got out and peered through the windows. I could see an old slate sink in the long kitchen, complete with an enormous wood-burning stove like the one Mom Nash had. I knew that stove would be great for baking. I stood there looking in and said to myself, *This is the house I am going to buy someday. I will raise my children here and have my family all around me.*

Beyond that wonderful kitchen, the house had a huge fireplace in the living room and an apple orchard on its fifty-five acres. I imagined raising sheep on the land. The idea of weaving wool from my own animals almost made me cry out loud. I wanted so much to live in this house, tending my sheep, dyeing and spinning and weaving their wool.

But the house wasn't for sale.

For years, I was patient and dogged, and eventually, the owners decided to sell. This house had become *my* vision, not my husband's. But the kids and I convinced him it was the right thing. I wanted to be a Mainer as much as I could be, and for me, this house in the countryside was a key part of the puzzle. I wasn't afraid to reinvent myself again. Part of me felt like I was coming full circle in Rockport and finally growing back into myself. I knew I could be happy here—no matter what Bill did.

It was a good house, and by 1973, we'd fully settled into it. Locals referred to us as "the hippies." I wore my hair long and loose and dressed in blue or black jeans with a black turtleneck. Bill was the local oddball artist who flew back and forth to Michigan for clients. We ate mussels, long considered junk seafood by the locals, for dinner, and I grew weird things in my large garden like garlic, arugula, celery, peanuts, eggplants, and melons, many of the vegetables that my grandmother had grown back in West Virginia.

There were garden doubters. My neighbor Milton was one of them. "Oh Marilyn," he used to like to tell me, "That garden of yours is not going to work in Maine."

But the garden *grew*, and I took great pleasure in bringing vegetables over to him.

All kinds of people gathered at our house for dinner or for a place to sleep. I had my loom, and I was taking care of four Suffolk sheep by now—three ewes, Sofi, Stella, and Stacey, plus the ram, Harold. It was a big job. The ewes would drop their lambs in the heart of winter, and I'd go out and help birth them. We had a menagerie of other animals too—three dogs and five cats and an extremely large donkey named Charlie, who hated Bill and would chase him all around the house with his lips curled back over his teeth. Occasionally, when Bill was out in the back field, I would see him running with Charlie close behind, head down, ears back.

Friends and guests questioned my sanity in acquiring Charlie. "Why a donkey?" The truth was that he'd been offered to us for free by some friends who were moving away. My kids had wanted a pony, but we couldn't afford one. The sheep made a little more sense to my friends because I used their wool for weaving my rugs, and I loved having the sheep. Still, they were always getting stuck somewhere.

Our neighbor Milton helped me put up chicken wire fencing to keep the animals confined to our property, but Charlie was masterful at getting out. Whenever he did, he'd head for the road in front of the house, where he would stand in the middle, refusing to move, even when a car came to a screeching halt right in front of him, horn blaring. Each time, I phoned Milton and asked if he could help me get Charlie back in and fix the fence. And each time, Milton said, "Just a minute, Marilyn." Then he'd hold the phone away from his face and yell to his wife, "Eleanor! Mrs. Moss's ass is in the road again, and I have to help her get it out."

Oh, how he loved that joke.

And oh, how appreciative I was of his help.

And oh, how I loved living in Maine.

My life was really my home. Cooking and taking care of the kids and animals. I chopped the wood. I spun the wool. I had no business ambition at all anymore. The only little bit of money I made was on sales from my rugs that I wove during the day on the sunporch when the children were at school. I loved this time in my life. But there was still that problem of money. Little was trickling in.

Chapter Twenty-One

The Little Wife

O ne night during the fall of 1975, Bill and his friend Dave concocted a new business idea over a jug of wine at our dining table. I braced myself. The old tensions between us had begun to fully emerge again. Bill took time now to light his pipe, then looked at me over his glasses. He knew I would be skeptical about any new venture. He'd formed so many different companies over the years, all dismantled now. He sat there at our table with his wild gray hair, wearing his blue jeans and large, black eyeglasses and L.L.Bean "canoe shoes," and said, "I think it's time we made and marketed our own tents instead of licensing out the designs to other companies."

Was that loud sigh from me?

He continued. "In this way, we could keep the quality and integrity of the design as it should be." He was still charismatic and able to easily win over investors with his ideas, but I was becoming much harder to convince. Still, it was true that the couple of sewing companies with whom we contracted didn't produce the quality we wanted, and occasionally, they changed details in the designs.

An enthusiastic and resounding yes came from Dave. "Yes!" he said again. "I had experience with sewing operations in California before moving east. We'd make a good team."

Me posing with a newspaper in a promotion for Moss Tents with Bill in the background.

Bill went to look for some more wine. I followed him into the cellar.

"Bill," I said, "I want nothing to do with this new company. I'll take care of the kids, weave, and pay bills, but I want no part of the idea. It sounds completely overwhelming."

He shrugged. "Suit yourself."

The next day, he and Dave laid out the steps to form Moss Tent Works Ltd. Then they convinced two men to each invest twenty-thousand dollars to buy used sewing machines, grommet-setting tools, and the raw materials to produce a few tents. One of these investors was Beac, my dear stepfather, who had retired and was living on a limited fixed income on North Haven with my mother.

Now I was worried—and rightly so. Within a few months, the two investors' money had been used up. Most of it had gone to salaries for Bill and Dave. Now this new company's total assets consisted of a few used Singer sewing machines, some tools, and two or three rough tent prototypes.

My stepdad was furious, and I was full of guilt. My husband had the audacity to borrow my stepfather's retirement savings. It may not have been an enormous amount of money to Bill, but to my stepfather, it was everything.

Beac came to our house one night not long after and said to both of us that he couldn't afford to lose that money. "Marilyn, I want you to get in there and turn this losing operation around."

I was the mother of two young children and had no manufacturing training. How could I possibly turn our situation around? Beac's belief in me was flattering, but how could I really help? The way I saw it, I had only two things going for me—I had learned long ago how to be a chameleon who could make myself fit in anywhere, and I had my daddy's can-do attitude.

But still. This was a stretch. Me running Moss Tents?

After Beac left the house, Bill sat with me at the table, smiling. "Sure, Marilyn. Why not? You be the president, and I'll be vice president of design."

I was furious. "Didn't I say at the outset that this idea wouldn't work? And you *never* should have asked Beac for money." I turned and went to bed.

But in the end, what choice did I really have? We had an overdrawn checking account. Unpaid bills piled high on the dining table. No savings account. And a very unhappy stepfather. Besides, I was Bill's wife. Right? Didn't I owe it to Beac to try to earn back the money that Bill had taken from him?

It was then that my daddy's voice came back to me, as it so often did.

You can do this, MarilynRae. Keep saying "I can do this. I can do this." And you will.

It was a turning point in my life, albeit not one that I ever sought. I've come to think that many of life's biggest changes happen this way—almost invisibly, while we aren't looking. And then the change is upon us. Overnight, my life was completely transformed.

I got up early and started the fire in the kitchen cookstove, beginning a whole different litany of chores than the ones at the farm in Elgood. I needed to fix breakfast, feed the animals, get the kids off to school, then head for the Tent Works factory where I was supposedly in charge.

Those first few weeks, I had a severe case of impostor syndrome and plenty of doubt. But I did not have any fear, and that distinction is worth pointing out. Fear could have stopped me. Doubt, I could live with and fake my way through.

The company was housed in an old wooden gunpowder mill on the edge of the Megunticook River in Camden. The building had two open concrete floors and a partial wooden mezzanine, with a main floor that had space for the sewing machines, a long cutting table, a shipping area, a reception office, a lunchroom, and a bathroom. The lower level accommodated the design and prototyping area, where Bill had turned one corner into his office and installed a large floor-to-ceiling glass window by the river "to see any trout swimming by." His fishing rod was always leaning against the door.

I began leading by using the intuition I'd gained during those years on my grandparents' farm. The work required perseverance, as well as the trust of Ted, my loan officer at our community bank, plus all the patient shareholders who believed in me and the incredible group of loyal and dedicated employees. But back in these days, just landing a few sales to retail shops was arduous. Shop owners and managers would tell me, "Never heard of a Moss tent," as they stood surrounded by products from The North Face, Sierra Designs, and JanSport.

Someone suggested that I try the "puppy dog trick." I'd put up a Moss tent in a shop showroom for free. When it sold, the retailer would pay for it and order another. It worked.

I traveled with tents to one outdoor retailer show after another. Ultimately, our products attracted the interest of independent sales reps and lots of camping enthusiasts. Each month, with a bunch of tent orders from backpacking dealers around the country in my hands, I would run to the bank for a short-term loan. I'd send the money to suppliers for materials and put the orders into production. As soon as we were paid, I'd rush back to the bank and pay back the note. Then the process would start all over again.

Probably the biggest mistake I made running the company in those early days was not knowing that an undercapitalized seasonal business required an asset-based loan. The camping tents were a seasonal business. The retailers submitted their orders in the late fall for spring and summer deliveries. We made them during November through spring and then filled reorders in the summer, so there wasn't any income during the fall and winter. Retailers had thirty days to pay their invoices, a deadline by which most of them didn't abide.

The company was always short on cash. But as our sales grew, I had to hire more employees, buy more sewing machines, and upgrade our hand tools so that we could take care of processes like applying grommets quicker and easier. And I had to keep learning. From weekend business workshops in Boston. From my employees. From trial and error. The Camden bank didn't have asset-based loans, so I had to acquire more shareholders, as well as a loan from Coastal Enterprise Inc.

My credo was to always be honest and trusting of each employee, to really get to know them. In the morning, I'd arrive on the sewing floor and stop to say hello to anyone I saw. I'd ask how they were doing, how their kids were. The biggest change that I brought to the company was my open-door policy. Anyone could come to me with absolutely anything. If you had a problem at work—any problem—or if you had a problem at home, you could come talk to me, and we would figure it out together. I believe that a policy like this creates the kind of work environment that allows people to thrive. Ours became the kind of work culture where everyone was seen for who they were. Everyone was appreciated for what they brought to us. No one was invisible or expendable.

One morning, as I walked down the row of sewing machines, talking to the women, I noticed that Crystal, who was hunched over the machine, pushing fabric through the needle foot, didn't look up. "Are you all right, Crystal?" I asked her.

She mumbled a faint, "Yeah. I'm okay."

I squatted down so I could see her face. A badly swollen black eye stared back at me. I also noticed her arm was bruised. "How about coming to my office in a few minutes?" I whispered.

No reply. She just kept pushing and pulling the tent pieces through the needle foot. But she came in a little while later, and I motioned for her to sit down. Then I closed the door.

"What happened? Are you hurt anywhere else?"

She lowered her head and started to cry.

As I handed her a box of Kleenex, I tried again. "Who did this to you?"

Many moments passed. Finally, she said, "I fell. I'm okay now. Thank you." She rose, put the Kleenex box on my desk, and went out the door.

Later that day, one of the other stitchers came into my office and blurted out, "Everyone knows her husband beats her. Has for as long as I've known her."

"Why hasn't someone done anything to help her?" I asked her.

"Like what? She doesn't want help. She always says she deserves it. She isn't about to leave him. And besides, where would she go, with no money?"

After she left the office, I was taken right back to that first night of my marriage in Chicago when Bill had hit me so hard that I fell down. I too had believed I was trapped because I had no money. I, too, had felt powerless. What had changed now was that I was in charge, and more and more, I was beginning to rely on myself and my own intuition. I was not looking to Bill or anyone else anymore for approval or permission. I believed that no woman should have to do that.

I called Social Services that afternoon, and the receptionist gave me the name for a domestic violence center with locations in Knox and Waldo counties called New Hope for Women. The executive director came to my office the next day, and I listened to what her organization did to find safe housing for abused women and children. Then I invited her back to speak to all of our employees, to make them all aware of the invisible violence going on in the homes around them. As a company, we learned how to better recognize domestic violence victims among our neighbors and friends and family, and how to get help to the person or child who most needed it.

A few days after this talk, a woman on the sewing floor named Marsha came into my office and asked for help. She said her boyfriend was hitting her and threatening to kill her and her young son. I urged her to move out of their house and call New Hope for Women. Two days later, at two-thirty in the morning, my home phone rang. Marsha was crying hysterically: "He came at me with a knife at dinner. I barely had time to grab my son and leave without a coat or my pocketbook."

"Where are you, Marsha?"

She told me she'd driven straight to a motel in Augusta but didn't have money to pay for a room. I told her to stay put until I could find her a room at a safe house with New Hope and then got the motel manager on the phone and gave him my credit card information. "Remember," I told Marsha, "Wait there until you hear from me or the director."

I called the police to get a restraining order against her boyfriend, and Marsha returned to work a few days later. I admired her resolve. After that, I was determined to help other women like her find the strength to stand on their own, to the point that some people in town knew me as Mother Bear, instead of the president of Moss Tents.

Besides my open door, I also now had a policy where employees could come to me if they needed financial help, for personal loans to take care of all kinds of needs—car and house repairs, really anything you could think of. I'd ask how much they could afford taken out of their weekly paycheck to eventually pay back the loan. No interest was ever charged, and every single loan I signed was repaid in full. It was this open, trusting work culture that built a confident, loyal workforce.

Meanwhile, Bill continued to churn out new design ideas, and almost every time, I told him, "No. Not now." Each time, I held my ground and explained yet again that we simply didn't have the money to try them. It caused a great deal of friction in our marriage, to say the least. The hardest thing I ever learned to say was "no" to my husband, but it was a lesson that was long overdue for me.

Now I was running the daily operations of the company, carting the kids back and forth to school, feeding the sheep, donkey, dogs, and cats, and cooking dinner on the wood-burning stove for friends who found corners in the house to put sleeping bags or erected tents in the yard. We always had guests staying over, and I loved it. I had not forgotten my time with Julia Child and her big-hearted cooking. I fully believed that food was love and that this was what Mom Nash had been doing all those Sundays on the farm when she got up at four to roast the chickens. I never stopped cooking, even during the hardest years at Moss Tents, when I was stretching and growing at the factory in ways I never could have foreseen.

Food was still how I relaxed. Cooking calmed me down and brought me back to myself. My menus were simple but satisfying, according to my most frequent diners, Jeff and Genie. Ragout was quite appreciated. Plus chicken *bouillabaisse*, beef stew, lamb curry, *pot-au-feu*, and *coq au vin*. We also feasted on lasagna, spaghetti carbonara, chicken Marbella, matelotes with haddock, hake, clams, mussels in white wine and herbs, and New England fish chowder, to name but a few. Most nights, I carried my thirty-pound Le Creuset iron pot filled with the evening dinner to the table, stepping over a carpet of sleeping dogs—an obstacle course that kept my biceps primed for any arm-wrestling challenge.

Back in those early years, Bill and I had an annual New Year's Eve party for about twenty friends in Maine, and I prepared for days, just like Mom Nash used to do. One New Year's Eve just before midnight, I announced that we would postpone dessert until after twelve and let Dimitri, our new Bulgarian friend, "do his thing." Dimitri's traditional contribution was to take half a loaf of my French bread, a little salt in a plastic bag, and a piece of firewood and run completely around the outside of the house and knock on the front door exactly at the first stroke of midnight to present me with "gifts for the new year"—bread for food, wood for warmth, and salt for good luck. However, this particular year, the snow was piled in four- to six-foot-high drifts around the house and still coming down.

It was rough going for him through the deep snow, but Dimitri leapt like an antelope, pushing through the snow until he came to the fence—and face-to-face with Charlie, who blocked him, mouth curved over his enormous teeth and ears flat back. Dimitri finally gave him a chunk of my bread and was permitted to pass. Then he dashed to the front door and almost fell inside when I opened it, just as the clock struck the first ring of midnight. He presented me with the gifts, a big hug, and my first kiss of the New Year. Bill laughed along with everyone else, as if we were a happily married couple. No one knew exactly how difficult he could be.

Although, as I found out later, I wasn't fooling most of our friends. As time went on, Bill's list of infidelities grew too long to keep track of. Some were with our employees, some with girls he met at bars. His professional infidelities mounted too, leaving behind a trail of angry clients and investors. My friends in town told me they'd seen Bill with one young woman after another. A mother of one of our young babysitters even called to say that her thirteen-year-old daughter wasn't allowed to work for us anymore. "Mr. Moss grabbed her breasts and pushed her up against a wall—thank God, she squirmed out." This put me over the edge, especially because Bill denied it.

One business partner told me Bill had prostitutes come to his hotel room whenever he was out of town on business trips. And in the midst of all this, he continued to drink, often becoming angry and irrational. My anger deepened, and I became depressed, which I hid from the kids and my employees as much as I could.

There was a stack of unpaid bills in my office down at the factory and a growing account of the company's losses. The feeling I had now was of failure—in the marriage and in the company and also as a mother, because I wasn't spending enough time with the kids. In bed at night, my thoughts often wandered to the idea of leaving, going anywhere at all. Just getting in the car and driving away with the children. But then my thoughts would turn to my own parents' separation. My fear was that Jeff and Genevieve would be desolate without their father. And then I'd think of the company—how could I ignore my obligations to the employees and the bank, to my stockholders, and to our clients and customers?

I was full of despair, but that didn't slow Bill down. Once, when interviewed by a local newspaper, the reporter asked Bill if he was the president of Moss Tents. "No," the article quoted him saying, "The little wife is. She's only seventeen inches tall." He thought this was hilarious.

My friends and I didn't.

This article was finally the thing, as Mom Nash liked to say, that "knocked some sense into my head."

I knew it was time to take full charge of both my life and the company.

Chapter Twenty-Two

I. Can. Do. It.

Each day, I went to work, trying to make our business turn a profit, which would not happen for years. At the same time, I carried more and more anger toward Bill as the bills piled up and our company lost more and more money. I tried to hide that anger from the kids and our employees. *Don't give up. Keep trying. I can make the company successful. I. Can. Do. It.*

Ultimately, Bill and I started leading separate lives. I took care of the kids and ran our business. He stayed with a friend in Portland and started another design company. I eventually learned that he illegally used some of the designs Moss Tents owned. I didn't have time to be miserable about any of this. I had a business to run, kids to raise, animals to care for, and a household to maintain.

When I woke up each morning, I wondered how in the hell I was going to make it through another day. My friends would ask, "How do you handle it all?" I don't know what answers I gave them, but I often fell asleep asking myself the same question.

At home, I had a pile of bills. At Moss, I had a pile of bills. I had payroll due. I had zero balance in bank accounts. What would I do now? One morning, someone came into the factory and said, "Have you tried to remortgage your home?"

I walked into the local community bank right after that and stuck my head in to the office of my loan officer.

"Hi, Ted," I said, as casually as I could muster, my heart pounding in my neck, "Have five minutes?"

I thought all bankers were like him, truly wanting to help. Because I did not let him down with my timely house payments and remodeled much of our first house myself, Ted listened to my plea. We remortgaged the house so I could pay off the Moss bills. He then suggested a new plan: I would bring in purchase orders, and he would loan the money for materials and labor. From then on, as soon as I received money from the camping dealers, I would pay Ted back.

I did a lot of running back and forth to the bank, purchase orders in hand one way and money in the account to meet that week's payroll when I returned. This worked—except when it didn't. Our dealers had thirty days to pay invoices, but most of them were small, and they didn't always make their payments on time. When those dealers were thirty—or even sixty—days late, I had to go and see Ted and explain. As long as I was honest and upfront, he let me slide.

But even with Ted's understanding, we still lost money every month.

"Marilyn," Ted said to me one Friday when I was borrowing again to meet payroll, "You've got to get help from the Maine Small Business Administration or from investors."

I got both.

And then I rolled up my sleeves, and got stubborn. I'd always played with the boys at school back in West Virginia. "Can you climb that tree?" The boys would often ask me. Well, of course I could. I wasn't raised on fear.

There wasn't enough capital or a business plan or proper and efficient machinery. In due course, we also realized that although our tents were beautifully designed, lightweight, and easy to erect, they didn't meet the performance standards of backcountry trekkers and mountaineers. Through outdoor sports magazines and our sales representatives, I contacted several top climbers and adventurers who agreed to test our tents and provide feedback.

We listened, and then we made changes: we added new reinforcements, better staking systems, different materials for ventilation and condensation, and new vestibules to provide more protection, as well as space for cooking and storage. We started classifying our tents according to the season. We pitched the lightweight, one-pole Solus as a tent for bicyclists to use in warmer months, while we sold the Olympic as a four-season, extreme-performance tent. It took several years, but eventually, our high-quality Moss Tents became a premier tent on the outdoor market.

Our tents were sold by Eastern Mountain Sports and REI, as well as by many small outdoor retailers across the country. We added the American flag and "Made in Camden, Maine" to our Moss logo on each tent, and we opened other markets by selling in Germany, France, Italy, and Japan. Slowly, week by week, our business started to gain traction.

So did I. With the sale of the camping tents, we renamed the company Moss Inc. And as Moss Inc. found its legs and began growing, I did too. It was leadership on the fly, but I was trusting all my instincts about how to create a successful, equitable company with a fair and honest work culture. Once we hit our stride, I did not look back.

Chapter Twenty-Three

"What's This Child Gonna Do Next?"

There is a story passed down in my family that I remember well, because I lived it. It's a story about how I ran away from my uncle's house in West Virginia in the dead of night when I was six years old because my aunt was hitting me. I ended up hitching a ride with a trucker. I was never scared. Foolish, yes. Reckless, sure. But not scared. And I think this story says something important, although a little hair-raising, about the value of not being raised on fear.

The story goes that my father had left me overnight with his brother Alex and his wife Ginny. Aunt Ginny bullied me and got a switch from the yard, pulled down my pants, and hissed, "You're a stupid, no-good girl, just like your father." I broke free, knocking her backwards, and ran out to the river, where I planned my escape.

After dinner, with a biscuit and piece of ham in my pants pocket, I went upstairs to the room I slept in and slipped out a window onto the highway, then held up my thumb as high as it would go. An eighteen-wheeler stopped.

"And what do we have here?" the driver said as he turned down the volume on the radio. "Shouldn't you be home in bed, li'l girl?"

I told him, "My Aunt Ginny's been beating me. I really need a ride to my Aunt Lottie and Uncle Frank's."

"Well, get in," he said, "and we'll see what we can do."

"How many wheels does this truck have anyway?"

"Eighteen. It's called an eighteen-wheeler."

I wiggled and pulled myself up and, with a hand up from the driver, landed in the seat. The driver said, "My name is Jimmy. What's yours?"

"MarilynRae."

"Okay, MarilynRae," Jimmy said. "Where exactly do your aunt and uncle live? Do you have a phone number for them?"

"I know they live in Hinton," I told him. "I don't have a phone number."

"Hinton. Where's Hinton. I don't know a Hinton in Virginia."

"Oh no. Hinton, West Virginia."

"Jesus," he murmured. He wasn't heading anywhere near that. "That's way up by Beckley."

"Oh. I'm sorry, sir," I said. "I'll get out and find another ride."

"Nope. Oh no you won't, li'l lady," he said firmly. "I ain't going to put you back on this dangerous highway. A li'l girl shouldn't be traveling alone, especially at night. How old are you anyway?"

"Seven," I lied.

Jimmy downshifted. "Well, MarilynRae, how's about we get ourselves a big fat hamburger?"

The truck slowed down with a blast of its air brakes and turned left into a parking lot filled with similar trucks. We got out at Mandy's Diner, and Jimmy put some change into the phone. I heard him asking for a number for my uncle. Then we ate our burgers and french fries, and I don't know how much time passed. The Mickey Mouse watch that my daddy had given me had stopped working long ago. But the diner door finally opened, and there stood my Uncle Frank with a worried look on his face.

"What the damnation are you doing, MarilynRae?" he said. "Trying to get yourself killed? Christ!"

After Uncle Frank thanked Jimmy and paid for our meal, I followed him out to the parking lot, quite pleased with myself. The problem of Aunt Ginny's bullying had been solved.

I climbed into the front seat, next to Aunt Lottie, who looked frantic. Uncle Frank got behind the wheel and said, "What's this child gonna do next?"

Chapter Twenty-Four

An Omen of Change

What I did next at Moss Tents was raise more capital. By now, the company had increased to seventy-two shareholders, but it was still carrying debt and had yet to turn any real profit. Then, one day, a simple phone call from a Pierre Cardin Shoes sales representative changed our fortunes.

The rep said he was tired of setting up the traditional, heavy wood-and-plastic exhibits at the shoe trade shows. He wanted a tent-like structure for his displays, and he wanted these structures to fold up and fit easily into a taxi. He needed, he said, to be able to set them up in a few hours, instead of two days—something more "like your camping tents."

Bill rose to the challenge, delivering three ten-by-ten-foot tent structures to an exhibit hall in Vegas and setting them all up in less than two hours. This caught my attention. I did a study of the trade show exhibit market and realized that our tent fabric answered all its needs. And this market was wide open. Soon, Bill's patented tension-fabric technology found a big market niche, and we were off and running, working with exhibit designers and builders all around the country.

Meanwhile, our camping tents had become internationally known, and in 1976, we signed a contract with an agent in Saudi Arabia and Pakistan to sell our tents to retailers, distributors, and to the military in both of these countries. Prior to this I had been looking for additional markets where we could actually make a profit. We hadn't broken even previously, our competitors were making their tents overseas and we had wanted to employ people who lived in Maine. This put us at a disadvantage. Soon, we were working with a Pakistani tent manufacturer that sewed tents, *by hand*, for the Pakistani army. This company licensed one of our larger tents, the Optimum 200, with a plan to begin creating them in Pakistan. But first they hired us to bring our patterns to Lahore and teach their employees how to make tents using the industrial Singer sewing machines we ordered for them.

"Us" in this case meant me, as president of Moss Inc., responsible for marketing, manufacturing, and financials; Bill, vice president and director of design; and Susan Willer, our expert in developing patterns and prototypes.

We flew into Karachi, then on to Lahore and stayed at the Lahore Continental Hotel, which catered to western tourists and businesspeople. The guests were all men. Every single one of them. I never saw another woman there during our entire three-week stay. Susan didn't seem fazed, but I was uncomfortable. Men stared at us. And, much to Bill's dismay, the hotel did not serve alcohol.

Each morning, our client sent a Mercedes limousine to take us to the factory, traveling miles through poverty-stricken neighborhoods. Hungry children reached out their hands, their desperate faces peering into the car windows at us. We often passed lifeless shapes wrapped in white cloths on the roadside—corpses waiting to be picked up and taken to a burning pyre. Arriving at the factory, we'd meet with the wealthy business owners. This staggering contrast was shocking. Every morning, I felt more and more embarrassed by my privilege and saddened by the poverty gap. The company's president, Mr. Hajeb, and its vice president, Mr. Ahmad, made it clear that they did not want us to mingle with any other Pakistanis while we were there.

Bill and I at the Moss facility in Camden in 1976. Photo courtesy of the *Camden Herald*.

Leaving our hotel at night, they insisted, was completely prohibited. "Mr. Bill, Mrs. Bill, you must not leave on your own at any time," they said. "We provide you with driver to take you to our beautiful sites and bring you to our factory and return you to your hotel. There, you have your dinner and stay."

Susan and I obediently stayed in the hotel most nights. But Bill, true to form, went off into the city each evening. I decided it was best not to ask him where he went or whom he encountered, and he never volunteered that information. To this day, I still have no idea what he did most of those evenings. As long as I kept Bill's and my relationship strictly professional within the company, the three of us made a fine business team, and I kept my sanity.

Bill was the seductive magnet, the entertainer—the genius and designer of great things. I was the negotiator, the "get the contract signed with payment" person. And Susan was the teacher. She rolled out the patterns and showed the all-male workforce how to cut the fabric on the bias to create the compound curves. After that, she taught them to use the Singer sewing machines, including the special attachment for a double-needle lap-felled seam. It was a major technological advance for the Pakistani company. Before this, each tent had been sewn by men who sat cross-legged on a dirt floor in a windowless room, one lightbulb above them, sewing every stitch by hand, pushing the needle through the thick fabric with their calloused big toes.

The company's managers thought that we Americans were a rare and perplexing curiosity. They couldn't understand how a *woman* could be president of a company. They also couldn't accept that Susan was what she appeared to be—a sewing and manufacturing instructor. Was she a mistress of Mr. Bill's?

With Bill, Mr. Hajeb stuck to business—discussing his designs, his design process, and other shelter concepts. But with me, the men mostly wanted to talk about personal things. One afternoon at the factory, Mr. Hajeb suddenly turned to me and asked, "Mrs. Bill, how often do you and Mr. Bill have sex?"

I was too startled to say anything.

Not that I needed to, because Mr. Ahmad immediately followed up with, "Does Miss Susan have sex with Mr. Bill?"

I managed to reply, "I don't know. Why don't you ask him?"

I hoped that this would put an end to things. But they wanted to know what positions we liked and what gave us the most pleasure. It was truly insulting.

Then Mr. Ahmad asked me, "Does Miss Susan ever join you?"

I finally told them my private life was not up for discussion. After that, I tried never to be alone with them. Each time I brought up subjects like the royalty payment schedule or payments for produced and sold products, their response was, "Mrs. Bill, don't concern yourself with such matters. It will all be taken care of. Our driver will take you to the bazaar today to shop."

I was feeling like the "little wife" again. *She's only seventeen inches tall.*

One night we had a dinner with a man named Zahoor, a well-known painter that Bill had met one night, along with his wife Scheherazade, a potter. Their dining table was long and narrow, and places were set for eighteen. It was a feast I will never forget. Colorful bowls and platters formed a solid line down the center of the table, filled with Tandoori chicken; *rajma chawal*, a bean curry; *makki ki roti*, a flatbread made from corn flour; *biryani,* rice cooked with vegetables and meats; and *chole masala*, a chickpea dish. Guests arrived at intervals, the last one taking his place in the empty chair on my left, dressed in the same white tunic and baggy pants as the other men but with a curved dagger in an ornate sheath hanging from a belt at his side. I said hello and held out my hand.

He nodded, shook my hand, and then turned away to converse with Zahoor in Urdu, where I heard the name Bhutto and the initials "PPP" mentioned quite frequently. Bhutto. Interesting.

Before we had left Maine, I'd read as much as I could find on Pakistan and learned that the Pakistan Peoples Party (PPP) was the progressive, social democratic party of Prime Minister Zulfikar Ali Bhutto, who'd been in power until General Muhammad Zia-ul-Haq ousted him in a military coup seven months earlier. I'd also learned that the PPP consisted mostly of Pakistan's intelligentsia, university professors, artists, and writers like Zahoor and Scheherazade. They lived with Scheherazade's parents, who were both professors at the University of Lahore.

Before dinner, I'd shown Zahoor a coin I'd bought on my trip to the bazaar. I liked its shape, with loops at the top, and thought that it would make an attractive necklace. Zahoor turned it over and over in his fingers. "It could be a very old Islamic coin," he said and translated the inscription on it for me. "It says, 'There is no God but Allah.' I don't know what period it's from." His expression hardened. "It should have some value, but there is a law in Pakistan that none of the artifacts from a certain period can be taken out of the country. This could be one of them. When are you and Bill leaving Pakistan?"

"Bill and Susan are staying a few more days, but I fly out tomorrow morning." I needed to get back to Maine to resume running our fragile company.

"Don't look so worried," Zahoor said with a beautiful, wide smile. "I'll make a cord and clasp for you, so you can wear it around your neck with your other necklaces. The agents at the airport won't notice it. Declare your other purchases and act nonchalant."

Bill heard us talking and came over and said, "No big deal. For Christ's sake, Marilyn, you paid for it. Fuck 'em."

But Zahoor took the coin into his studio and came out a short time later with it dangling from a cord made of many silk threads, their ends secured by wrappings of leather strips looped through a silver hook and ring. I turned around so he could fasten it in the back. "Now, tuck it under your other necklaces," Zahoor said. Which I did. "There," he said. "It looks lovely, and unnoticeable."

That night, as soon as we got back to the hotel, I became violently ill. I spent hours on the bathroom floor with a fever and chills, crawling on and off the toilet. The next morning, on the way to the airport, my driver told me what had happened the night before in Lahore. "Maybe another bloodless coup," he said. "One never knows for certain what's going on. And the militia plan to hang former prime minister Bhutto today. A lot of people upset."

My mind flashed back to the dinner party.

As we approached the airport, I saw many armed men gathered around the entrance. The driver moved past them and pulled to the curb. "Last night," he told me, "The Pakistan Peoples Party, angered by the lack of promised elections, started an uprising. General Zia-ul-Haq put an end to that and declared martial law again." He looked at me in his rearview mirror. "My advice, Mrs. Bill? Don't trust anyone." Then he got out, opened the door for me, put my bags on the curb, and drove off.

I checked in at the gate as invisibly as I could, keenly aware of the nausea and the possibly illegal coin around my neck. The ticket agent smiled at me as she handed me my ticket. "You will board at 9:15. But first, you will go with my colleague into a private room. For your safety and the safety of others, you will remove your clothes and she will check you."

Whoa. *What have I gotten myself into this time?*

A middle-aged woman in a uniform appeared beside me, touched my shoulder, and pointed to a door. I gulped and followed her. The room was much like a changing room in a department store, with a small desk and a chair. "Undress, please," the uniformed woman said. "There is no need to remove your underwear."

Her expression was stern as she looked me over and patted me down. I did not remove my necklaces or the silver loops on my wrist and arm. The coin lay flat, somewhat concealed under the turquoise stones of another larger Native American necklace. She glanced briefly at my jewelry, then looked in my eyes. "Are you sick?"

"I'm feeling nauseous and weak. May I sit down?"

"Of course." She pulled the chair out from behind the desk and motioned for me to sit. "I just need to ask you a few questions, then you can get dressed. Please show me your passport."

She asked the usual questions: "Where are you from? What was the purpose of your stay in Pakistan? Where did you stay? Where did you go? Who were you with?"

The driver's words flashed into my head: *Another bloodless coup. My advice, Mrs. Bill? Don't trust anyone.*

"Just our business clients," I said. "We stayed in our hotel at night."

The agent raised her gaze from my passport and moved it to the bottom of my throat. My heart hammered. I almost reached for the coin. *Maybe she'll just take the coin and let me go. Or maybe I'll be taken to jail.*

"All right," she said. "You can get dressed. Your flight leaves soon."

I dressed quickly and headed for the bathroom. Bile was rising in my chest. Whatever illness I had, it was getting worse. When our flight was announced for boarding, no one paid any attention to the agent calling out row numbers. Everyone hustled and pushed their way forward toward the doorway. Instead of a line, it was a throng. I was grateful to find that my aisle seat was near a bathroom. As I slumped down, waves of nausea roiled from the bottom of my stomach and pushed up through my chest. Even my eyeballs and teeth hurt. A flight attendant walked past, took one look at me, and brought me a glass of water, a blanket, and a pillow.

The flight was supposed to take twenty-nine hours from Lahore to New York City, with stops in Karachi and Dubai and a change of planes in Frankfurt. Things went according to plan until we arrived in Germany. Then, because this plane had left Lahore, where there was political unrest, no one was allowed to get off the plane. In fact, no European country would let us land. By the time we touched down in America, toilets were overflowing and the flight attendants had run out of water. I felt so lonely. So very much on my own.

Eventually, we landed at JFK in a snowstorm. I felt the coin, cold against my skin. *Could it be that the coin was cursed? Or was it my lucky charm?* The trip from Lahore to Maine, took forty-one hours.

I found the sight of my mother and Genie and Jeff at the Rockland airport so heartwarming that I burst into tears.

When Mom saw me, her eyes widened. "We're going straight to the hospital."

I stayed in the hospital for two weeks while the CDC tested for malaria. The doctors injected one anti-malarial antibiotic after another into me, hoping one would do the trick. Finally, one did.

Over and over throughout those two weeks, I reached to my neck to make sure the coin was still there. It was a foggy, hazy time, and the coin reminded me of the embarrassment I had suffered because of the men there and how I would no longer take that kind of humiliation. Not from any man. Especially not from Bill. But some part of me also wondered if this might be a lucky coin. It had gotten me home. Maybe the coin was actually an omen of change? Because change was coming. I could feel it.

Chapter Twenty-Five

Crash Landing

B y 1982, Bill had fully abandoned ship. Meanwhile, the company had grown from three employees to thirty-nine, and sales had increased dramatically. The problem was that our balance sheet still showed losses of more than five hundred thousand dollars. However, our board of directors remained supportive and encouraging. They all saw that the company was on track to become profitable, and they said so. One of them, James Rockefeller Jr., went a step further.

James, whom everyone called Pebble, was from what he called "the poor branch" of the Rockefeller family. After a board meeting that fall, he called me on the phone. "Marilyn," he said, "you looked exhausted today. I think you need a diversion. Maybe a hobby. It would help you to get your mind off the business every now and then."

"Are you telling me to take up knitting?"

He laughed.

"No. Something intense and completely apart from your everyday routine—like having an affair. Or taking flying lessons."

I was so startled that I didn't say anything. After a few seconds, I found my voice. "Well, I don't know anyone who's looking to have an affair. Besides, this town is too small. Everyone would know about it within a day."

"Would you like to take flying lessons? I can loan you my plane. I know a good instructor. My only requirement is that you take out insurance."

I had never thought about flying, and I had to mull it over. During the next few days, the idea grew on me steadily. I started imagining myself up in the sky alone, with a white scarf streaming from my neck. Amelia Earhart. Why not?

I showed up for my first lesson at the hangar, located next to a grass airstrip by Pebble's house in Camden. He and a very tall instructor stood beside a tiny white plane with red stripes, waiting for me. I had never seen the plane, the airstrip, or my flight instructor before. Suddenly, I was terrified and almost turned the car around to leave. I parked about twenty feet from the plane, waved to the men, and did my best to look brave, but for a few seconds, I was too frightened to get out of the car.

The airstrip was scary enough. It sat on the side of a hill with a pond at the end and mountains on two sides. Then I looked closely at the minuscule plane. Its nose was pitched up in the air. Its tail rested on a small wheel on the ground. Two tiny seats were positioned in the incredibly narrow cabin space, one in front of the other. How would we ever fit in there? The instructor looked to be at least six foot six. He would have to fold himself into three equal sections to fit into that plane. My kneecaps quivered.

The two men must have seen the horror on my face. They smiled, walked to my car, and opened the door for me. The instructor's waist came to the top of my doorframe. He leaned down and said, "Hi. I'm Manning. Let's get started."

Ten minutes later, I was sitting in the front seat of the plane with Manning piloting in the seat behind me. Pebble stood watching on the edge of the airstrip. We taxied slowly to the top of the hill while Manning walked me through the final preflight checklist over the headphones. Then we took off.

Within seconds, my kneecaps stopped shaking, and my body was overtaken with a surging thrill. Fear was replaced with what I call a true sense of ebullience. I was rising above it all—above Bill, and the debts, and the stress, and the depression. All the ugliness slipped away as the plane climbed higher into nothingness.

The next week, I took another lesson. I read every biography on female pilots I could find. I quickly grew very fond of Pebble's little plane, a Piper Super Cub with skin made of thick fabric, stretched over a steel frame. It had a control stick instead of a steering wheel and was called a "taildragger" because of the way the tail sat on a small wheel, tilting its nose up. Wherever you were, in the front or the back, you couldn't see where you were going when the plane was on the ground. I had to learn to use the right and left rudder pedals with my feet, swerving the plane in a zigzag fashion in order to see where I was headed on the runway.

Pebble and I preparing to take off in his Piper Super Cub from Camden in 1982.

On the third lesson, I flew the plane on my own, with Manning's close guidance. It required total concentration and I was terrified. But Pebble was right. There was no way I could think about any of my problems while flying.

The more I flew, the more I loved it, and the stronger I felt. I was MarilynRae again, meeting a dare from the boys back in West Virginia and climbing the highest tree. I flew higher and higher. I took the ground flying test and got all the questions correct.

After eighteen hours of flying instruction, I soloed. I couldn't believe I was up there in the sky, all by myself, conquering the challenge. I was hitting the can with a bullet. I was climbing into the cab of a stranger's eighteen-wheeler. Just as Pebble had suggested, my anxiety lessened, and leading the business became easier.

After a total of seventy-three hours of flying, Manning told me I was ready to take the Federal Aviation Administration test for my private pilot's license. Two days before the test, I was on the production floor of the company, talking with the supervisor and two of the stitchers about the week's production scheduling. "Marilyn, you have a call on line two," the receptionist said over the loudspeaker.

I headed for a phone. It was Manning: "This couldn't be a better day for you to practice your touch-and-go landings. Go get Pebble's plane," he said, "and do it." He spoke rapidly, as if we couldn't waste an extra minute talking about it.

"I'm sorry, Manning," I told him. "But I'm right in the middle of working on our new production schedule. Plus, I have a gruesome deadline to meet for next week and need to get the purchase orders to the bank for another loan before it closes today. I'll practice tomorrow."

To my surprise, his tone grew angry. "Come on, Marilyn, do you want to be a pilot or not? Tomorrow it's supposed to rain. You need to practice. Today's the day." He paused. "The sun is shining, no wind—it's perfect." Then, in a softer tone, he said, "Get to it, gal."

"Okay, Manning. I'll do it."

"Haste makes waste," Mom Nash used to say to me when I was ready to run out the door. But I didn't have much time. After calling Pebble to confirm that the plane was available, I grabbed my pocketbook and jacket, jumped in my car, and headed for the airstrip.

When I got there, Pebble was pushing the plane out of the hangar. I thanked him, climbed into the cockpit, closed the door, and opened the window. Then I pushed the starter, moved the throttle forward a little to get the engine revving, and watched the propeller move from a slow turn into an almost invisible spin.

I taxied up the grass airstrip to the top of the hill, turned the plane around, went through my final preflight check list, and closed the window. With the throttle pushed full forward, I rushed down the hill. Halfway down, I pulled back the stick and became airborne over the pond. Pebble stood by the hangar and waved his red handkerchief as I climbed up over Ragged Mountain.

The view was spectacular—two hills on either side, with the fall foliage reflecting on the water. Manning was correct. The sky was clear, and there wasn't a breath of wind. It only took me about ten minutes to fly to the Knox County Airport. There wasn't another airplane in sight. I had the place to myself. I announced on the radio that I was going to practice touch-and-go's, then turned on base for grass runway number 21, pulled back the throttle, and started the descent. It felt perfect. My plan was to land on the grass strip, as I had done many times before.

It was a beautiful landing. *Manning will be so proud of me.* I used a little right rudder to see to the left of the plane. To my shock, the plane had swerved off the grass strip into the adjacent tall weeds. I pushed the left rudder. The plane went up on its nose, then dropped gently back down onto its tail as I heard a faint sound of fabric ripping. It sounded like I had raised my arm and torn the underarm of a tight cotton blouse.

I heard a car speeding toward me. It pulled up to my right, and George, the local plane mechanic, hopped out. Everyone who flew planes around the area knew George. He was a superb mechanic and an old friend of Pebble's, with long, stringy gray hair under a soiled, crumpled leather cap and an equally long, stringy gray beard and mustache. When he wasn't working on airplanes or cars, George was an artist—a potter—and a great storyteller. He yanked opened my cockpit door and stuck his head in.

"Jeezus, Marilyn. Are you okay?"

"Of course," I said to him calmly.

George looked at me like I was an imbecile. Then his gaze moved to my left side. I turned to see a tree branch protruding through the cockpit floor, halfway up to the ceiling of the plane.

"If you'd landed just an inch to the left, you'd have been a fuckin' popsicle," George said.

"Oh my God!" I grabbed hold of the door.

"Here, let me help you out." George reached under my arm and back.

"I'm fine, George. Really. I can get out myself."

I climbed out of the cockpit, then looked back. The plane was a mess. The propeller was bent. The wing spar was broken.

My legs threatened to buckle under me.

"You did a damn good job messin' it up," George said, taking my arm and leading me to his car. "I saw you come in. It was a perfect landing, but you were just a little too far right and on the edge of the grass. When you used your right rudder, it pulled the plane into the tall grass. Then, when you used the left rudder, the wheels couldn't turn in the tall grass. This made the plane go up on its nose. The only problem was that when it fell back down, it landed on the *only* tree branch anywhere near. You're a fuckin' lucky lady."

George loved to swear.

He paused, took out his handkerchief and blew his nose, and pointed toward the car.

"Well, get in. Where's your car—at Pebble's?"

I nodded. My thoughts were tumbling in my head, trying to undo the accident. Then, my mind turned to Pebble. *Oh my God. I've destroyed his plane.*

"I'll drive you back," George said. His car was a mechanical Frankenstein's monster. He didn't believe in buying anything new, so the contraption was put together out of pieces of many other old, crashed cars. Engine and axles from one. Fender and windows from another. Hood from another. It was sort of a collage art piece.

"No, wait a minute, George." I looked at him. "I have to report the accident to the FAA. I better get my logbook out of the plane, and then I'll call the FAA and Pebble. He'll be getting worried."

After retrieving my logbook, we drove over to the small terminal, and I made the call to the FAA and reported my accident. The male voice on the other end of the line asked me a string of questions, and I answered each one honestly and thoroughly. Then he said, "Ma'am, don't get discouraged. You survived. You'll be a better pilot because of your accident. Get right back in a plane tomorrow."

Was he kidding? No way. My knees were still shaking.

My next call was to Pebble.

No answer.

I called Manning next, and I could tell he was alarmed. But his words echoed the guy from the FAA: "Well, we'll have to get you right up there in the sky again tomorrow. You'll need to rent the airport flying club's plane, a Cessna 150. Remember, you still have your flying test on Thursday. You and George drive over to Pebble's house. I'll meet you there."

"Come on," George said. "Pebble's probably standing out on his airstrip right now. It's approaching dusk, and no one can land there in the dark."

On the drive over, all I could think about was how I was going to face him. It was such a special plane, and Pebble loved it.

It was getting dark when George slowed to round the corner near the house, and a car came up behind and rammed into us. My seat broke loose, which knocked me forward, and I hit my head on the windshield. George's seat also broke loose, but he managed to pull the car off the road, where we opened our doors and threw ourselves out.

George hurried over to my side to see how I was, and we looked at one another in disbelief. Then we both started laughing.

"George," I gasped, "I've never been in a car accident. I've never been in an airplane accident. Now, I've been in both within the same hour."

The driver who had hit us was standing by her car, crying and holding her wrist and saying over and over, "I'm so sorry . . . I'm so sorry . . . I didn't see you."

George looked at her wrist and felt it gently, then said, "It's broken. I'd better drive you to the ER." He turned to me. "Marilyn, you walk on up to Pebble's place."

I was somehow still alive. In shock and wobbly, but in one piece. My neck and head hurt, which I knew would make the two hills on the way to Pebble's house feel impossible to climb, but I started out, nonetheless.

By now, it was pitch dark, and I felt panic take over as I tried to think of what I would say to Pebble. I hadn't walked far when a set of headlights came up behind me and stopped. I heard a car door open.

It was Manning.

"Thank goodness!" I said, hurrying to get in. We drove in silence up Pebble's driveway. The house was dark, so we went out to the airstrip, where we saw multiple lights on either side of the runway.

"My God," Manning said.

As we got closer, I saw what Pebble had done. He'd parked every vehicle he owned—his snowplow, his tractor, his backhoe, and his two cars—along the landing strip and turned their lights on, trying to outline the runway for me.

Our headlights caught sight of him walking toward us with a flashlight in each hand.

I rolled down the window and said, "Pebble, I'm so sorry . . . I crashed your plane . . . badly . . . at the airport. I feel terrible. I'm really sorry."

Pebble glanced at Manning, then looked at me as he leaned on the window. It seemed an interminably long time before he spoke.

"Machines can be replaced," he said finally. Then he paused, and I could see that his eyes were wet. "Good people can't."

A strong emotion came over me then. *This man cares for me more than his plane.* I think I was seeing him for the first time, realizing that there was something genuine between us.

That night, I had a dream that I stood on a green, grassy hill beneath a deep blue sky and saw a plane flying above me. Suddenly, it turned its nose toward the earth and dove, crashing into a nearby hill. There wasn't any noise. Everything was quiet. The plane stood vertically on its nose, partly buried in the ground. Then it wasn't a plane anymore and became flames that shot straight into the sky, like a bonfire. I could see a figure of someone inside the flames. I walked closer to see who it was. I recognized the figure. It was me.

That night, I also discovered splinters going all the way up my left side—into my leg, my hip, and my arm. At the hospital the next day, I had X-rays and a brain scan, and a nurse removed all the splinters. My brain was fine, but whiplash from the car accident had dislodged my fourth and fifth cervical vertebrae, which were causing the disk to bulge.

That dream haunted me for a few days. Was it a harbinger of a tragic accident? *Should I never fly again? Should I change my unhappy life? That figure in the plane—was it the old me that I am finally ready to leave behind?*

Three days later, I rented the Cessna 150 plane from the flying club, and after Manning checked me out in it, I flew it over to Augusta to meet the FAA agent for my pilot's test. I performed all the required air maneuvers and made a perfect landing, passing my test with flying colors. I felt calm and peaceful the whole time I was flying. I knew I could do it. It was like my daddy was right there with me in the plane.

When the agent and I returned to the Augusta terminal, Pebble and Manning were both waiting for me. Pebble handed me a dozen red roses and gave me a congratulatory kiss on one cheek. Manning kissed the other cheek. I felt higher than I'd been in the plane!

Chapter Twenty-Six

A Declaration

That summer, when Pebble invited me to his daughter's wedding, I said yes. I wasn't at the reception long before he asked me to dance. He wasn't a smooth, fancy dancer like Bill, but the closeness sparked something in me. I left the reception right after that, feeling shaky and filled with longing for him.

The next morning, he called to say he was planning to fly the newly repaired Cub over to Vinalhaven Island where his daughter and new husband and friends were continuing the celebration. Would I go with him and drop a bouquet of flowers for them out of the plane? By now, the bond that I sensed growing between us both thrilled and worried me. He was still married and living with his wife, although the marriage was breaking up. But I couldn't resist the invitation—both to fly and to be with him.

He'd picked a huge armload of wildflowers from his field, which he placed in my arms after I climbed into the Cub's rear seat. "I'll fly low," he said, "and do several passes to let them all know we're there. Then I'll signal you when to open your window and make the drop."

We passed over the cove, and everyone shouted and waved when they saw the plane. I threw the flowers, and they fell among the people on the shore and floated out on the water. It was a beautiful thing to watch, and this father's sensitive gesture for his only daughter grabbed my heart.

As we flew up and out of the cove and headed back toward the Camden hills, I felt the wind drying my tears. I knew I was falling in love with him.

A full year after my plane accident, in late June 1983, Pebble appeared in my office one morning and asked for a lunch date in the park. "I've brought two sandwiches," he told me. "And a bottle of wine."

I didn't know what to think. The two of us weren't in the habit of having lunch dates. What was he up to?

In the park, he told me that he'd fallen in love with me two years ago but had been too shy to come forward because I was still married. It was only now, he said, after he'd found out that Bill had truly, finally, left the company, the children, and me, that he dared to speak of it. He was also married, but called that relationship "the worst mistake of my life." He was miserable and the marriage was coming to an end.

That day he said that he wanted to marry me.

I wasn't sure I'd heard him correctly. The wine and the proposal had left me giddy. *Had he really just asked me to marry him?*

He said it again: He wanted to marry me and take care of my children and me forever.

I'd never felt more loved and cared for than I did in that moment. Nor had I ever dared to imagine this day would happen.

Pebble reached in his pocket and brought out a tiny square box and held it out. Inside was a simple, thin silver band.

"Read the inscription," he said.

I read it out loud: "To Bunny. With love, Pebble—1952."

"Are you familiar with Margaret Wise Brown?" he asked, looking at me.

"Of course," I told him, smiling. "She wrote *Goodnight Moon*. I started reading that to my kids as soon as they could sit up. They loved her books."

Pebble nodded. Then his expression became serious, almost grim. "She was my fiancée," he said. "My beloved. We were engaged to be married in June of 1952, but she died of a blood clot in France that March."

I was stunned. "Pebble, I had no idea—"

"I gave her this ring for our engagement, before she left for a book tour in France and I began a sailing trip around the Pacific. We were to be married upon her return, and she was wearing this ring when she died."

He slipped Margaret's ring on my finger now, professing his love to me forever.

"This was the ring for my first deep love. Now I give it to you. I love you and want to live with you for the rest of my life."

Tears streamed down my face. Were they for his lost first love or for my happiness? I think, both. I had never felt so in love before.

The ring fit my finger perfectly, which stunned both of us.

"Must have been meant to be," Pebble said.

George, our resident bohemian plane mechanic and sage, was right: I was a fuckin' lucky lady.

Chapter Twenty-Seven

Are You Pregnant?

I filed for divorce and Bill came home to Rockport soon after, professing his enduring love and devotion to me. As we sat at the kitchen table on the morning he came back, his mood switched from anger to his old charm, and, soon, he was trying to woo me again.

"Let's go somewhere exciting for a week," he said. "Get away from all of this. You'll regret it if you leave me for Pebble. It's the money, isn't it? Instead of a struggling artist, you want money?"

He was pacing the room now, looking half-crazed.

I felt a sense of calmness and shook my head. "It's too late, Bill." We had already discussed all of this, too many times—how our marriage didn't work and how miserable I was. "You chose to leave me, remember?"

I took his arm, escorted him to the door, and gave him a gentle nudge. Then I locked the door behind him. His mood swings were starting to scare me.

After this visit, the kids cried and yelled at me for leaving Bill. How could I do such a thing to him—and to them? Jeff was seventeen and Genevieve thirteen. I could only tell them that I loved them and that I hoped they'd come to understand my decision.

Once it was clear to Bill that I was forever beyond his reach, his earlier promise of devotion and love turned to anger again, and he threatened to kill us both. I took some clothes and moved into a house that Pebble had rented for us.

He had his own version of suffering in this love affair of ours. His wife was not happy at all, even though she'd been estranged from him for some time. She called me on the phone and told me that I was making a terrible mistake to be with Pebble.

"You know," she said, "he is a very peculiar man."

"Thanks for the warning," I told her. "I'm sorry." Then I hung up.

These two breakups were known all over our small town—the four of us were the gossip of the moment. Friends took sides. But after Pebble's divorce came through, I moved into his house. I'll never forget that day.

As Pebble drove me up his long, steep driveway, anxiety swept through me. Although I had visited there many times, this trip was different. Pebble's home was now my home. It was a tall, two-story, red clapboard farmhouse from the 1850s, connected at a right angle to a larger wing, where, for many years, Pebble and his crew had built wooden boats, and stored cars and planes. The whole structure looked overwhelming, like the kind of mysterious compound you might expect to see on a TV western. All I kept thinking was that I didn't belong there.

But inside, the house was smaller and more manageable. The foyer had a brick floor with a stack of cut firewood, each piece carefully placed. A turn to the right led into a little kitchen with dark wood walls and a low ceiling. Even with its bay window, under which sat a table and two chairs, the space was dark, in part due to a wall of shelves. There was an olive green electric stove and matching olive green refrigerator. The two treasures in the kitchen were the ornate, cast-iron Jøtul and an antique Norwegian cupboard.

How was I going to cook in such a dark, small space? I'd always had a big kitchen where we'd all hang out, cooking and talking, just like on Mom and Dad Nash's farm. The kitchen was the heart of a house for me. And an electric stove?

But Pebble didn't want any change. I began to feel that I was competing with two ghosts for Pebble's attention and love. The first was Margaret Wise Brown. The second was Liv, his first wife and the mother of his children. After Margaret's death, Pebble met Liv Heyerdahl in Norway, where they lived for three years before moving to the farmhouse. Liv died of cancer there in 1969. Her photos and possessions were still strewn throughout the house. Despite these ghosts, I somehow needed to turn the house into my own nest.

After much discussion, Pebble finally agreed that the kitchen was small and dark, and a renovation took place, both literal and perhaps figurative. Soon we had a large, bright kitchen, both beautiful and functional. Pebble ended up loving it.

However, out on Vinalhaven Island, where Margaret Wise Brown had left her house to Pebble, everything remained the same. He was devoted to his memory of Margaret, and this old love of his began to build a wedge between us.

I kept silent about it at first, although thoughts of his devotion to her ate away at me. I wasn't sure how I'd be able to deal with it. Eventually, I would come to understand that he could keep his love for Margaret in his heart and still grow his love for me. It took patience, one of my inheritances from the Nash family farm. Thankfully, I had lots of patience, and I was willing to work hard, both at running my business and at building my new marriage.

When I shared my fear of the two ghosts with Pebble, he said that he understood. It was the beginning of both of us really learning how to communicate in a marriage, truthfully and honestly. I had never done that before.

I had grown up a poor Appalachian girl and was about to marry a member of America's most famous family—and one of its richest. Pebble was shy, liked to stay home, and had a slight aversion to entertaining. I loved cooking and having crowds of people over. I also loved music and couldn't imagine living without it, but he mostly liked silence. At first, we both indulged each other's likes. Then, we let the pretense go and gave each other space and respect for our individual likes and whims and entered a truly wondrous stage, where we created a fifty-fifty relationship, with full support for each other in all our passions.

As for the ghosts, the more I learned about each of these women, the more my jealousy turned to respect and fondness. We loved the same man, and this crucial realization connected me to them in a special way.

During my divorce, Jeff and Genevieve remained angry with both Pebble and me. Bill convinced them that I'd abandoned him to run off with a rich man, and he filled them with stories about how dreadful I was. He also presented himself to the kids as a poor, struggling artist and a victim. Of course, he was the one who walked away from me. Nonetheless, for a time, Genie and Jeff didn't understand that I was going to marry a man who genuinely loved me and whom I loved back. Their anger, thankfully, didn't last long.

Over time, they learned more about their father from friends and family members and began to understand how unhealthy their parents' relationship had been. They began to show their love for me again, and they found love for their stepfather, who was humble and kind to them. He became the caring, engaged father they'd never had.

My children attended boarding schools, but returned to Pebble's house to stay with us during vacations. They also spent time with Bill in Portland. By this time Bill and I had put our house in Rockport on the market to sell.

It wasn't long after I moved into the farmhouse that Pebble took me to meet his parents in Greenwich, Connecticut. Before we drove down to their house, he'd written them a tongue-in-cheek letter announcing that he had "changed the administration."

They were not amused. In fact, the letter shocked them.

Pebble was fifty-seven years old by now, and I was forty-three, but as we pulled into the Rockefellers' long, asphalt driveway, dread filled my heart. I felt like the sixteen-year-old version of myself again, meeting my prom date's parents. We entered the property between two stone pillars that opened to a circular, brick courtyard. The house itself was also brick—an enormous Federal with a large wing jutting out on the right side.

"Wow," I said to Pebble. "That's some house."

"That wing to the right is the servants' quarters," he told me as we got out.

Pebble's mother Mrs. Rockefeller, or Nan as I came to know her, welcomed us into the entry hall and gave me a chilly handshake and a look that said, *Who has our oldest son brought home now?* By this time, I'd learned more details about Pebble's former flames: There was Margaret Wise Brown, beautiful, worldly, sophisticated, and much older than he was. Then there was Stella, a lovely Tahitian woman he met while sailing in the South Pacific, with whom he'd fathered a son. Next was Liv, the adventurous older woman he'd met in Norway and married. Liv, the ex-wife of Thor Hyerdahl, was the mother of two children with Pebble. After her death, there had been another wife. All he ever said about his last marriage was that it had been based on poor judgment on his part and hers.

Did Mrs. Rockefeller think I was just another woman on Pebble's long list? A temporary romance of sorts?

She announced that tea would be served in the library at four o'clock, then excused herself to talk with the cook and her staff about dinner. I remember thinking that Mom and Dad Nash's whole house would have fit into their foyer. Pebble took my hand then and led me into the library—a lovely, high-ceilinged, wood-paneled room with two floor-to-ceiling windows offering views of the expansive lawn and flower beds. Several birdfeeders hung from tree branches, with birds and squirrels scurrying for the seeds. A large pine desk jutted out from the wall, and a painting of Mrs. Rockefeller in her younger days—dressed in Carnegie plaids on a hunting trip in Scotland—hung over the huge fireplace. The butler had already laid the logs in the fireplace for Mr. Rockefeller to light at cocktail hour, which Pebble informed me would be promptly at six.

As I scanned the room, I realized with a start that someone else was already there with us.

Mr. Rockefeller, Pebble's father.

He sat in his khaki pants and khaki shirt, slumped in a well-worn dark green leather chair, his large hands resting on his knees.

"Dad," Pebble said, "this is Marilyn."

I put out my hand. "It's a pleasure to meet you."

He did not get up. Both his hands remained on his knees.

I retracted mine.

Then, he said in a booming, startling voice, "Are you pregnant?"

"No, sir. Rather impossible."

I was forty-three, and my once-cancerous uterus had been removed when I was thirty—plus Pebble had had a vasectomy long before I'd met him.

"Are you Jewish?" Again, his voice was loud and demanding.

"No, sir. I'm part Native American, though."

"That's not too bad," he said, a little more softly and reached out his hand.

As time went on, Pebble's father—whom everyone called Bee—and I developed a great rapport. He told me that I was his favorite "outlaw" because I actually worked for a living.

Chapter Twenty-Eight

Lady, You Make Crap!

When I think back on the life span of Moss Tents and my time there, two men were instrumental in my learning curve. One was Harry Harding (1903–1998), my first business and marketing mentor. In the 1960s, he'd served as vice president of the Young & Rubicam advertising agency in New York City and, later, as a senior executive for Time Inc. Harry always had time for me. Besides giving me key marketing advice, he created our official name—Moss Inc.—as well as our logo, stylized from my signature. Harry said that the branding of the logo—the "trademark," as it was called back then—"was the key to good and successful marketing."

In a hand-scribbled note from 1983, he wrote to me, "Always attach the logo to every piece of fabric—it needs no further identification—it means 'Moss made this.' When alone on a printed page, it means nothing—yet! Someday (hopefully), the reader could see it and say, 'They make the best tents in the world.'" Amazingly, it was a prophecy that came true.

Then there was Roger Street, a tall, lanky consultant who walked into the Moss factory one day in the spring of 1996 unannounced and asked to see me. In doing so, he changed the course of our company forever.

Our receptionist, Eleanor, buzzed my intercom to tell me he was there, adding, "Marilyn, I think you'd better come right down. He seems very nosy, looking around everywhere."

I was irritated by the interruption and hurried downstairs, but Roger wasn't waiting in the reception area. Instead, I found him in his cowboy boots, pressed jeans, and requisite blue shirt with the sleeves rolled up, looking under the sewing tables.

When he saw me, he walked over, a huge smile on his face. "Roger Street here," he said as he stretched out his hand and gave me a firm handshake.

I was not interested in his charm. It was a busy morning. "May I help you? I'm Marilyn Moss."

"I know. An investor and trustee of your company told me I should come and meet you."

He pushed his large glasses higher up on his nose.

"Oh, really? And why is that?"

"Well, he said your company is losing money. Is that right? I help businesses turn around, from loss to profit."

I raised my eyebrows. "I could certainly use the help, but the company can't afford a consultant right now. I do appreciate your coming by."

I turned away, but he grabbed my arm.

"I know all that. Just listen. Here's the deal—I've recently retired, and my wife and I moved to my family home in Cushing. My two sons are grown and off with families of their own, and I want to give back to the state by helping businesses in need, such as yours." He made a wide sweeping gesture at the sewing floor with his long arm. "What I'm saying, Marilyn, is that I won't charge you a dime."

He gave me a short spiel. He'd worked in a Toyota factory in Japan where he'd learned something called the Total Quality Management process. Using this training, Roger then worked for the Jacuzzi company, turning it around from big losses to profits, and then did the same for several other struggling US manufacturers.

"Please," he said to me. "Show me your operation for a few minutes."

His pitch sounded like hype, and I had a lot of work waiting for me on my desk. But I agreed to give him a cursory tour.

The Singer sewing machines were humming. The grommet machine tapped rhythmically. Our cutter was on his knees up on the long table, using the fabric saw to cut through thick layers of nylon fabric. We had thirty-six employees then, and they were all busy working. I pointed to them and said, "Hikers, mountain climbers, and campers from all over the world write and call to tell us that we make the best tents in the world."

Roger peered at me through his glasses. Then he said loudly, "No, you don't. Lady, you make crap!"

I froze in my tracks. Heat crept up my neck and face. Then I asked him to leave immediately.

"Wait." The big smile reappeared on his face. "Let me explain. Look over there at the shipping table. You're letting only quality go out the door. That's good. But you spend money on inspection and then lose more money putting the mistakes aside, increasing your losses. Somewhere along the way, the process isn't working right. Those tents that you shelve and store as seconds and those not repaired that you keep under tables are costing the company a lot of money, just sitting there. Your inventory is killing you."

My mind was on fire. How dare he say we made crap? He had no idea of the complexity involved in the making of these beautiful, functional tents. He had no idea how hard we all worked.

He shoved his hands into his pockets, watching me closely.

As politely as I could, I thanked him for coming and told him I had to get to the bank before it closed.

He paused, waiting for me to say more. But I simply turned to go back to my office. As I walked away, he said, "Well, it's been nice talking with ya."

That evening, over dinner with Pebble, I told him about Roger and how he'd infuriated me. "What does he know about how to make a tent? His clients made cars and Jacuzzis. Our technology is complex. He didn't even see our financials. How does he know how much is carried in inventory?"

Pebble sat quietly listening, eating his dinner, and occasionally nodding and letting me go on and on. We'd been married several years and always openly shared our opinions on each other's projects. Pebble was always calm when I ranted.

"Marilyn," he said now, "I think you should at least find out more about what he has to say, don't you? It's not like you to not listen, or to walk away from anything."

He was right. And despite my complaints, Roger's words stayed with me throughout the rest of that evening: *Lady, you make crap . . . You're letting only quality go out the door . . . Your inventory is killing you.* He'd talked about how our losses were piling up and asked why we had to set up and inspect every tent if it was the best in the world.

You must put quality into the process if you're ever going to make a profit, he'd said.

I could still hear his words as I tried to go to sleep that night. Hmmm . . . maybe he had a point.

I called him back the next morning and began by apologizing.

"No problem," he said with amusement. "That's the first reaction I get from everyone."

We scheduled an appointment for the following day. "Set aside a couple hours," he said. "I have to start with *you.*"

That morning, Roger appeared at the factory right on time and bounced into the front office with a huge smile on his face. "Good morning, Eleanor," he said to our receptionist, then stopped to get a cup of coffee in the lunchroom before bounding up the steps two at a time to my office. He sat across from me at my conference desk, turning and twisting, crossing and uncrossing his long legs, trying to get his long frame comfortable.

"These chairs are meant for ladies with small bottoms and short legs," he announced.

Then we began.

He called it my education in Total Quality Management. It would end up being the path to my company's full success.

"In this training," he said, "I start with the president first, and if he or she listens and trusts me, we include the managers. And then we go to the production employees, the ones who know exactly why they're making mistakes. But unless you and your management team buy into the process, Marilyn, and become involved right from the beginning, it won't work."

Chapter Twenty-Nine

The Light at the End of the Tunnel

A t first, the entire sequence that Roger suggested sounded ass-backwards. "We start," he said to me that first morning in my office, "by getting rid of that sign you have up over the sewing and patterning room." He was referring to the one that said 100 TENTS OR 100 LASHES.

"I didn't put that up," I said, laughing. "The employees did that in jest when they were told that they needed to produce one hundred tents per week to meet our delivery dates."

Roger shook his head. "Maybe there were a few weeks when they came near this goal, but at what cost? How many tents went into the defective bin?"

I didn't have an answer for this.

"You're going to replace that sign," Roger said. "The new sign will say: 'Do it right. First time. Every time.' We'll start with the goal of only five tents per week. All perfect. No seconds. If any tents have defects when they're inspected, throw them in the dump."

I gulped, scowled, and let out a huge sigh. "That's sacrilege— to throw away a useful tent that could be repaired and then used by someone! Anyway, I thought you wanted to get rid of inspections?"

"You *will* get rid of them—but not just yet. And you'll only be throwing tents away for a short time. Until we develop trust that the quality process is working." He gave me that giant smile again. "This learning and changing process is going to take time, and it will be costly," he admitted. "But it will all pay off in the end. Threefold or more."

Taking risks. Trial and error. Wasn't that my usual style of learning? And trusting? Limiting production as well as adding more expenses were difficult decisions, based on trust. But the more time I spent with Roger, the more I believed in his process and in him. Making the changes was hard for everyone. But isn't change usually hard?

First, Roger spent a few days walking me and my department managers through the whole process. I had to run to keep up with his fast stride. Up and down the stairs and back and forth to the inspection and packing and sewing tables. Then I introduced him to Ted, the man who inspected each tent before it went out the door.

Roger said, "Okay. Let's start here, so I can see what all the defects are. Ted, why don't you inspect a tent as you normally do and show me any flaws."

Ted pulled a tent out of the cart and set it up. "This is a four-season Olympic tent. One of our best." Ted then climbed up on the table and crawled inside the tent. He showed Roger how he scrutinized the tent each time before it went out and felt with his fingers along each seam. Then he zipped and unzipped each zipper on the rear window and front door before he crawled back out. Next, Ted walked around the table, checking each single and lap-felled seam of the tent. He felt and looked for fabric flaws and discoloration from the dyes, and he inspected both sides of each tacked webbing tab. To my disappointment, he discovered a flaw.

"See here?" he said. "The stitching doesn't catch all the fabric."

Ted inspected more tents while Roget watched, one tent after another—and found flaws in almost a third of them.

"Too much fabric grabbed in the seam."

"A missed tack, but this can be easily fixed."

"Look at these gobs of thread on one side of a tack."

"Here, an oil stain from one of the machines."

"A flaw in the fabric."

"The binding isn't caught in the seam."

With each flaw that Ted discovered, Roger raised his eyebrows. "Ya don't say," he said each time, turning to look me in the eye.

Finally, after Ted had inspected thirty tents, Roger said, "So, now what happens?"

"I'm pleased I didn't let these tents go out the door," Ted said proudly. "This run of thirty tents is going to our top dealer. We need to go back and make repairs where possible."

"Ya don't say." Roger had his hands in his back pockets now. His pointed elbows stuck out like a bird getting ready to take flight. Out of the thirty tents Ted inspected, nine were defective.

Ted said, "If a flaw is something the stitchers can fix, I put a note on it and put it in one of those boxes under the counter, by the sewing step. Some have too many flaws and can't be fixed well or they'll end up with needle holes. Those I fold, putting a tag on the tent bag saying what the defects are. They get sold locally as seconds. We price them according to how bad the flaws are. The ones without flaws, I fold with poles, stakes, and instructions, and put in boxes, ready for shipment."

"Oh my God!" Roger whispered in my ear. "We've got a lot of work to do. Where's your tacker?"

I pointed to Roberta, working at the tacking machine.

Roger picked up one of the defective tents and brought it to her.

"Good morning, Roberta," he said, giving her his enormous smile. "I'm Roger Street, and I'm doing some work for Marilyn here. Do you have any idea why some of these tacks are perfect, but then there is this one?"

"Sure," Roberta said. "I'm so short that I can't reach the pedal without stretching my leg and foot out. Most of the time I hit the pedal okay, but other times my foot slips off or I lose my balance and stay on it too long."

"Ya don't say?" Roger squatted down to look at the pedal and Roberta's foot. "Well, we can sure fix that." He looked at me. "I'm going over to the frame shop. I'll be back soon. Don't go away."

He returned a few minutes later with a block of wood and a roll of duct tape. He crouched and taped the thick wooden block onto the pedal.

Then he said to Roberta, "How's that? Can you reach that pretty easily?"

"Oh, yes," she said, smiling. "Thank you. That's much easier."

"Good. Now, another thing—Ted said sometimes there's one or more tacks missing. Why's that?"

"There are so many tacks on some of the tents like the Big Dipper that I lose count."

"Well, that's another easy one."

Roger turned to Joanne, our sewing supervisor, sitting just a few feet away. "Ma'am," he said, "please make a note to buy Roberta a counter-clicker. Have Bob fasten it to the tabletop close to Roberta's hand. She can tap it every time she makes a tack. Tape a card to her tabletop listing exactly how many tacks she needs to put into each model."

Roberta seemed pleased.

Almost magically, two of our ongoing problems had been identified and corrected—at close to no cost.

But Roger wasn't done.

When I came home that evening, I shared the events of the day. Pebble agreed that the changes sounded logical and smiled when he said, "I knew you could do this."

That night, lying in bed, I thought of how different my life looked now. Pebble and I were wholly honest and committed to one another, and my confidence had grown exponentially. I trusted myself now, which made me able to trust change and all the innovations someone like Roger wanted to implement.

"Where's that machine for lap-felled seams?" Roger asked me the next morning on the sewing floor.

I pointed to Suzie, our head seamstress, and Roger and I walked over to her machine. I introduced the two of them—but at this point, everyone on the shop floor knew who Roger was. In fact, they'd all stopped working and were staring at us in mild amazement.

Suzie kowtowed to no one and always spoke her mind.

Well, here goes, I thought.

"Show me what you're doing," Roger said to her.

Suzie looked at him and, in a defensive manner, said, "I've been sewing for years, even before Moss Tents."

"Ya don't say?" Roger said. "Excellent."

He watched her take the edges of the layers of fabric and feed them into the feller, an attachment on the sewing needle foot that folds and makes two seams of stitching. As she worked, she explained each step and each movement.

When she was done, Roger lifted up the fabric and looked along the seam. He pointed at an area where the fabric was caught and wrinkled.

"Why does this happen?" he asked her.

"Oh, that happens sometimes. The pieces aren't the same length, and I have to fold some extra fabric into the seam."

"And why's that?"

"Different cutters, I guess."

Roger rubbed his chin. "Sounds like a pattern issue. And what about the gobs of thread that Ted showed us?"

"This machine gets out of adjustment quite often."

"And then what do you do to fix it?"

"Oh, I can't fix it. We need Bob, our machine repairman, and he isn't always around. So, I either take a break or find something else to do."

"Oh, brother," Roger muttered softly, and raised his eyebrows at me. "Thank you, Suzie."

He pointed me back to my office, and as we left the sewing area, I could hear everyone whispering to one another.

Roger grabbed another cup of coffee from the lunchroom, then came into my office and closed the door.

"You know what? You're teaching your employees to make mistakes. And you let them *continue* to make mistakes, because they think you can still make money with the seconds. Which, of course, isn't true." He stopped to take a big gulp of coffee. "No one has asked them why they have trouble always making a correct seam. You're losing money right and left, and you're not letting them make quality."

I felt my face turning red from embarrassment. I knew Roger was right on all counts. I had been defensive at the beginning, when he first dropped into our lives, but I'd always appreciated learning from my mistakes and from listening. Maybe because I'd just gone through some enormous changes in my own life, I knew how good change could be.

So, I was all in on Roger's plan.

He gave me another one of his big smiles. "Don't worry, Marilyn. When I come back tomorrow morning, we'll talk to the cutters and pattern makers. These problems are all solvable."

I felt invigorated. There was a lot of work ahead, but we had a shared goal, and soon we'd have a direction and a plan. A small painting by a Maine artist named Dozier Bell hung on the wall in my office. I called it *The Light at the End of the Tunnel* because I was always able to draw hope from this painting. It seemed like a harbinger of the company's future to me now. The light was becoming brighter.

Chapter Thirty

Making Hard Decisions

R oger came into the factory day after day that year of 1996 to, in his own words, "turn over rocks and see what crawled out." He found one problem after another, many of them easily fixable at little cost. The cutting machine needed a sharper blade. Some of the patterns were not accurate. Flaws on one side of the fabric sometimes weren't visible when the cutter unrolled the long pieces on the table. Once the simple issues were resolved, he brought together middle management to set up task teams for the bigger stuff.

In some instances, we found another easy fix. Others required us to purchase new, better equipment. Now our goal at Moss was being realized: *Do it right, the first time, every time, on time.* It became our mantra. When Roger told all of us at our next company-wide meeting that our new goal was to cut and run only five tents at once through production, some of our production people gasped audibly and laughed.

"I'm serious," Roger said. "We're going to keep making only five per run until we can get all of them finished—with zero flaws. If Ted finds even one flaw in a tent, it will be put in the dump."

"*What?*" everyone exclaimed.

"Roger," Ted said, "when we fix the minor things, we have a perfectly decent tent for someone to use."

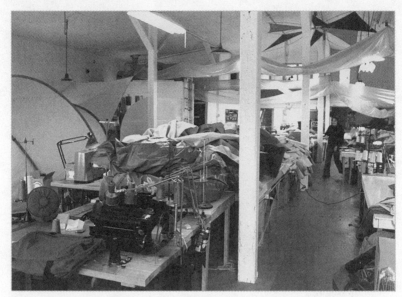

Moss production at the Camden facility in 1992, before Roger's Total Quality Management training.

Moss production at the Camden facility after Roger's training.

"That's not doing things right. Do you want that to be your credo: 'Moss Tents—Perfectly Decent?'"

It was a hard lesson, and it took two years, but by 1998, we had all finally converted to the "quality religion," as Roger called it. He taught us how to better organize our production schedules and processes, so that we all knew exactly where we were with each tent and each order at any given time. He showed us, too, how to build more collaborative relationships with suppliers of quality fabric, zippers, and poles.

I learned an incredible amount during those crucial two years. And I grew along with the company's growth.

"I have to compliment you, Marilyn," Roger said out of the blue one day, almost exactly two years after he started advising us. He was looking through our purchase orders and production run sheets, which he'd laid out on my desk. "You've generated an admirable company culture here. There is respect for you and for one another. I sense a great loyalty. Everyone wants to do a good job and to make the company successful."

He was right.

After all our tireless work and the patience of my board of directors and the shareholders, we'd finally, proudly, increased our productivity by thirty-six percent. The bad news was that, at almost the same time, Maine's unemployment tax increased substantially, wiping out most of those gains. Meanwhile, our competitors—The North Face, Sierra Designs, and JanSport—had one by one reduced their costs by moving production overseas. Now, most of the other two-person tents sold for $150 to $200 less than a Moss Tent. I was confronted with the hardest decision I'd ever had to make as the CEO.

Since we couldn't even come close to competing on price with our competitors, we either had to also move production overseas or sell our camping tents division. It was a terrible choice. Moving production out of Maine would have left all our employees high and dry, and I was never going to do that.

Our tension-fabric sales for the trade-show exhibits had been profitable for the past two years, and that department was growing like wildfire. I saw that if we sold off the camping tent division, we'd still have a thriving exhibit company—just a smaller one. But one that didn't include our iconic Moss camping tents—the seed for the entire company. It was a hard, hard moment.

But after many sleepless nights and many discussions with my directors, I chose to sell our tent division to REI for five hundred thousand dollars in cash. The sale felt right. It was still incredibly difficult, but it enabled us to buy a much-needed larger facility in Belfast, Maine, where we continued to grow and create ever bigger tension-fabric exhibits.

The same process that we'd used to revolutionize the backpacking tent market at Moss was now the very one we used with our new tension-fabric technology. We also used the same lightweight nylon materials and shock-corded aluminum poles at the exhibits. These exhibit fabrics folded into small bags and were much easier to install than traditional wood and Plexiglas exhibits. When the fabric got backlit in the exhibit halls, it was wonderfully distinct from the other exhibitors and stood out like a fantastic jack-o'-lantern.

Today, there are copycats, but Moss stands in front when it comes to exhibit fabric, grossing over fifty million dollars in sales, all because of the company's trusting work culture and commitment to excellence.

Now that we had a larger facility, I began making other changes to increase worker satisfaction. I set up a workout and wellness room and hired a trainer to come in once a week to work with any employee who needed help creating and maintaining a workout routine. I brought in a yoga instructor during morning and afternoon breaks and offered employee programs in healthy weight loss and smoking cessation. I also added programs for domestic abuse awareness. At first Roger raised his eyebrows at these programs, but eventually, he saw their benefit as absenteeism dropped considerably.

It was a continuous learning environment, but we kept increasing productivity and putting quality into the process, eliminating inspections and the dreaded seconds. The process of "Do it right, the first time, every time, on time" was now ingrained in our workplace.

Roger continued to be involved at Moss, but came to the facility less regularly. Then, on July 12, 1999, my bedside phone rang at two in the morning. My heart raced, as any person's would, hearing the phone ring in the middle of the night. The voice was barely audible. It was Bruce, one of Roger's sons, who lived in Atlanta. I strained to hear him.

"Marilyn," he said. "I'm sorry to call at this hour, but I know you would want to know. Roger was killed in a two-vehicle crash on his way home from Augusta tonight."

When I got to work that morning, a stunned silence greeted me. Someone had shared the news with the staff, some of whom had tears in their eyes. We all gathered in the large setup room to honor him. Roger had garnered such respect at Moss that I couldn't imagine the facility without him. I owed him so much. I had taken risks all my life, but Roger had instilled a greater confidence in me. I was so lucky to have worked with him. On that sad day, I asked everyone to share what they wanted to say about Roger. It was a long session.

Many times in the coming year, I would hear myself say, "Well, Roger would tell us to do it like *this*." It was difficult to look over at the empty chair in my office and not see him trying to fit his large, tall frame into it. I missed him and his unwavering honesty: "Lady, you make crap."

Chapter Thirty-One

Doing Good

Another man came to Moss Inc. soon after that, sort of like an oracle. I don't remember who introduced Gus to us. He was suddenly there, at Pebble's and my house for dinner one night. A big man, tall, with a large head and wide smile, who knew of my company and wanted to visit.

"I hear you recently bought a large facility in Belfast and sold the camping tent division?" he asked me. "You know," he went on, "I consult with businesses to help them create mission statements. I would love to do that with Moss Inc. How about it?"

He didn't even wait to hear my reply.

"In fact," he said, "I could do the work in the next two days. It would give me a little time to snoop around."

That was how I found myself with all forty-some employees, sitting in a large circle in our setup and patterning room, all of us holding large yellow pads and pens. There had already been a few groans, and now the metalworkers rolled their eyes and shook their heads, ready to leave.

When I reassured everyone that they were still on payroll, their expressions relaxed. But it took a while for Gus to convince them that creating a mission statement was not a game and would instead prove to be a crucial tool to help us build an even more successful company.

"Now," Gus said, "I am going to ask twelve questions, which you should each answer as honestly and thoughtfully as possible, with just one word or a few. Okay?"

Many of us shifted in our seats in confusion as Gus fired his first question: "Why do you come to work?"

I would say that "stunned" was our overall response. Was he kidding? Was this a joke or a trap?

Finally, some brave soul said, "To make some money, of course." All the heads nodded.

"Fine. Then write that down." Gus paused. "After that, write down the answer to question number two which is, 'Why? Why is that?'"

"Why is what?" asked another employee.

We were all trying to understand what he wanted us to do.

"Well, why is making money important?" he said.

I found that even I was groaning. How could this exercise get us all on the same page and produce a good mission statement? Then it dawned on me as I looked at my single word answers— with every question that each of us answered to ourselves, our company values were sprouting and taking hold.

After a few more minutes passed, I sensed the resistance shifting, like a train slowly picking up speed. Everyone's heads were down, and their pens were moving rapidly on the paper. Even the guys who usually scoffed at many of my ideas, like having the yoga teacher come in during break time to offer instruction, were on a roll. I liked to think that they trusted me now and that they had become attuned to the values and beliefs that I led the company with— the same thing that had guided Mom and Dad Nash at the farm: Listening. Hard Work. Humility. Good instincts. Pride in the work. Then add Daddy's dose of fearlessness and can-do attitude.

When everyone had finished, Gus gathered up the papers. "I know you had to trust me, or at least Marilyn, to participate in this, and I thank you. What I will do now is read through them all and list the words you used most. This will tell us all what kind of a work environment you want to come into. It will tell us what makes you feel good at work. What makes you feel needed. What makes you want to do your best work."

The list was astounding to me. The same words kept appearing again and again: Trust. Respect. Appreciation. Good pay for good work. Caring. Tolerance. Pride in the product.

From there, we gathered suggestions for the mission statement, keeping in mind that this was to be a living document, typed on one page, not carved in stone: a paper for each employee to keep at their desk, machine, or work area to be used in all aspects of doing their job and working together.

It would consist of 1) a section for the process, end-product, and client; 2) a section for employees; 3) a section on community and our involvement; and 4) a section on environment. A committee of volunteers was formed to create the employee section of the mission statement, with at least one representative from the sales and marketing group, the financial office, the design group, the frame shop group, the pattern and sewing group, the purchasing and inventory team, and the shipping and inspecting team. After two weeks, a rough draft emerged, and after more meetings, a consensus was formed. Kent Price, who handled public relations, composed the final draft, unanimously approved by our employees.

After this, we started referring to the mission statement whenever conflicts arose or whenever we were addressing new projects or new clients, new markets, new suppliers, or any discrimination issues. We learned how to use our new tool to better inform clients, suppliers, job applicants, and the community what Moss Inc. really was. Whenever someone was interviewing a new job applicant, they would give a copy of the mission statement to him or her and say, "This is who we are here at Moss." It was an environment where there was tolerance for differences and no tolerance for intolerance.

At this point, Moss was increasing its sales and hiring new employees. Other business leaders in the state often jokingly asked me why it seemed like I was "getting all the good applicants."

"Imagine," I replied, "wanting to work in a pleasant, caring environment."

I was often asked how I'd learned to run a company. After all, I didn't have any business training. I always answered that I led by using my values of trust, respect, and caring without discriminating against any religion, ethnicity, or sexual orientation. When one of my male employees applied for medical insurance for his partner and was denied, I'd called the insurance company and said that if they didn't put his male partner on the insurance, I not only would cancel my company insurance with them, but I would encourage other small businesses in Maine to follow my lead.

The insurance was granted. As far as I know, Moss was the first company in Maine to provide insurance for gay couples.

As our company became a state role model for a successful, socially responsible business, I was invited to speak at different for-profit and nonprofit conferences on various themes, ranging from human resource management to effective leadership. I always tried to address the main *How* question at these talks: "*How* do you achieve loyalty and pride in a workforce by being socially responsible but still manage to become profitable?"

I always thought of Roger, and of Daddy, and of Mom Nash. Leadership, in my mind, was simple. It was all based on respect and trust.

By 1999, we had 164 employees and annual sales had reached fifteen million dollars, with customers all over the world. Best of all, we were turning an excellent profit, year after year. I often needed to meet with dealers all over the States, as well as in Europe. We had a distributor in Japan and a marketing office in Germany. The travel was often grueling. But whenever I left the house for the Portland airport, there was a sealed envelope waiting for me on top of my briefcase with the words "Marilyn—Do not open until at 35,000 feet" written on it.

I'd stuff the envelope into my briefcase and carry it onto the plane. Then, once we reached cruising altitude and clouds floated below me, I'd open the envelope. Inside was a love note or an original poem from Pebble. It made me smile every time.

It would take years of counseling and studying Zen meditation before I let go of the anger and guilt that ate at me over my marriage to Bill. Even though I was divorced and happily remarried, for years, I still sometimes wished Bill harm, or even death, until he died of a heart attack in 1994. He had managed to become a monster to me, just like he had to his own son and to Jeff and Genevieve.

Living and working with him had been like a high-wire act, and it took a toll on me. No matter how hard I tried, I couldn't come up with a good explanation for my hasty marriage to him. As much as I loved being independent and strong, it seemed, for a while, that I needed a male in my life. Had Bill been a replacement for my daddy, who'd been missing for most of my young life? Had I been looking for a father figure?

So, when I was urged to write and publish a book on Bill and his work, at first, I turned away. "But Marilyn," a former employee said, "a guy in New York City is talking about doing one. If anyone presents Bill's work, it should be you."

The two years that I worked on my book *Bill Moss: Fabric Artist & Designer* were filled with many agonizing moments, reliving my turbulent life with him. Creating a tribute to this man was a struggle for me. But in the end, I discovered that by writing that book about Bill, focusing on his designs and not on his tragic flaws, I had worked myself out of my anger.

183

Chapter Thirty-Two

The Ghost of Margaret Wise Brown

After more than three decades at Moss, I knew I needed to move on and let someone else take it to the next level. So, in the fall of 2000, I sold the company to a group of investors for fifteen million dollars. The buyers told me that they bought us because of our committed, loyal employees, our respectful workplace, our quality products, and our socially responsible approach to business.

On my last day of work, in 2001, I was presented with a black book with a red Moss logo on it. Inside, each employee had written their personal comments. It was only when I got home that night and read them, that I surrendered to the tears I'd fought hard to hold back throughout the day.

Here is just one entry that echoes all the other 163 heartfelt notes:

> I would never have stayed at Moss so long (twenty-four years) had I not felt the respect and been respected and enjoyed the people I worked with and felt proud of the products that I put out. You made us believe in ourselves and that anything was possible. Every day we are aware of that. I hope we continue to make you proud, as we are proud of ourselves.

Following the sale, I collapsed into a depression. No longer was I a cheif executive, working sixteen-hour days. My identity had been Moss Inc., and if I was not Moss Inc., who was I?

It took me two years to fully recover.

The turning point was when I started getting up at four, making a cappuccino, and sitting by the fireplace to write down any thoughts that swirled in my mind—from feeling sorry for myself to the simple description of the sunrise on the sculpted snow; from anger over Bill that I thought had long been resolved to fantasizing about renting a house in Italy for a month; from reeling after the long years of work and sacrifice and trials to thinking about starting a new business. *Oh no!*

I poured my true emotions onto the page, and the depression subsided. Now turning thoughts into words on paper became an obsession—the reason to get out of bed every morning. I *wanted* to write. It didn't take long to realize I needed to learn more skills, so I went to graduate school and worked toward a master's degree in creative writing. When it was time to write my thesis, I knew I needed a quiet place, away from the activity of our Bald Mountain home.

Pebble suggested that I stay at The Only House on Vinalhaven—the house Margaret Wise Brown left to him when she died. "You'll be alone to do your work," he said. The Only House was certainly private. Margaret called it The Only House because at night, she couldn't see any other lights.

On a crisp day in November 2008, Pebble loaded his boat with a supply of food and took me and our Norwich terriers, Oliver and T. S. Eliot, across Penobscot Bay. In the afternoon light, the small, two-story wooden house looked especially inviting, snuggled against the vertical ledge that Pebble said, "was Margaret's whale."

He and I had built a screened-in porch off the house, which extended out onto a huge granite ledge. The tiny house itself had only three small rooms—a kitchen, a combination sitting room and office, and a bedroom, which was filled completely by the wooden bed in which Pebble had been born in New York City. Otherwise, The Only House was filled with all her things. And, as I soon discovered, her ghost.

The interior was exactly as she had left it. There was a maple desk snuggled into the wall under a bow window, where Margaret sat, facing the sea and the small islands, writing many of her books. A small, faded Victorian couch filled the corner. Another green velvet Victorian chaise sat along the wall. A bookshelf hovered above the chaise. A black iron Franklin stove barely fit into the remaining corner space. The small, rectangular kitchen had a narrow, four-burner gas stove and oven and a gas refrigerator. At the end of the room, there was an old oak drop-leaf table with two chairs over which hung a magnificent, elaborate red glass kerosene lamp. It was a singularly lovely and solitary place to write, and I hoped I'd made the right decision to come.

Pebble and I carried my supplies up to the house. Then he blew me a kiss and departed. Oliver, T. S. Eliot, and I stood on the deck, watching the boat back away from the dock, with Pebble waving. Then I went back inside, unpacked, and set up my traveling solar panels. The little house didn't have electricity, so I connected the panels to a twelve-volt car battery to charge my laptop. Next, I organized all the research notes for my thesis on the desk beside my laptop. By now, the sun was beginning to set. The dogs and I went back out onto the deck, where I sat with a drink and smoked a small cigar. We watched as the colors changed in the western sky and birds flew home to their nests. I thought of Margaret enjoying the same view, a drink in one hand and the pipe she liked to smoke in the other, an image Pebble had often described to me. I felt her presence then—the presence of a kindred spirit.

As darkness engulfed the cove and the house, I went inside and lit the fireplace and the two red kerosene lamps. Shadows formed on the walls as the flames flickered. I opened my laptop to begin work.

A sudden tenderness ran down my left arm. Was that a hand on my shoulder? Oliver emitted a low growl, and both dogs' heads and ears perked up. I turned quickly, but of course no one was there.

As the days and nights passed at The Only House, I often fingered Margaret's ring as I worked. I was grateful to her and Pebble for making it possible for me to be a visitor at this magical place. I also reread some of her books, which were shelved in the sitting room, the same books that I had read to my children when they were young. When I looked out the large bow window above her desk—which was now *my* desk—I imagined her writing these words in *Little Island* as she sat gazing at that same spot:

> Nights and days came and passed
> And summer and winter
> and the sun and the wind
> and the rain.
> And it was good to be a little island.
> A part of the world
> and a world of its own
> all surrounded by the bright blue sea.

Many days as I wrote, surrounded by fog and the songs of seagulls and terns, I felt the gentle pressure of her hand on my shoulder. The dogs were no longer startled by her ghost. Sometimes the fog shrouded everything, and I couldn't see a single thing out of the window. It was as if the rest of the world had disappeared, and my dogs and I were sharing The Only House with Margaret. Her presence seemed so real to me, so encouraging.

I sat and wrote about how I'd looked to find myself through others for so long that I'd lost touch with my own needs. I wrote about how I put "li'l MarilynRae" in a room at the farm and closed the door. About how I needed to bring her fully out now and integrate her into my new life.

I saw myself then on the porch swing in Elgood—a little, spirited, fearless MarilynRae. The mountain girl who always sought belonging had grown up. She now had her own courage and strength.

Chapter Thirty-Three

Coming Full Circle

O n December 9, 2011, I sat in a chair by my dying
mother's bedside at the local assisted-living facility,
where she'd been suffering from dementia. Her diagnosis
of Lewy body dementia, diagnosed years before, had gradually
progressed to the point where she could no longer receive the care
she needed at home.

Months earlier, she'd slipped out the facility door, and I'd found
her standing outside in the parking lot. "Where are you going,
Mom?" I'd asked her gently, taking her arm to lead her back inside.

"I have to get to the top of that hill." She pointed her arthritic
finger. "Daddy will be waiting to take me home."

There was no way I could stop my tears from springing forth
now, because she really was going home, while I sat by her bed and
watched her slowly die.

"The world is round and the place which may seem like the end
may also be the beginning." This is a quote by Ivy Baker Priest, the
thirtieth treasurer of the United States of America, who mobilized
female voters to support Dwight D. Eisenhower in his 1952
presidential campaign. However, I prefer T. S. Eliot's version:

What we call the beginning is often the end
And to make an end is to make a beginning,
The end is where we start from.

Eliot's words are more active. If we expect anything to change, then we, as individuals, must take responsibility and make it happen. So it was with my mother. So it has been with me.

I held her limp hand and gazed at the shallow movements of her chest, dreading that last one. Her face was relaxed and tranquil, her skin smooth and luminous, appearing much younger than her ninety-three years.

"Mom," I said, "do you remember that time when Bill Randall taught us how to fly-fish in the Connecticut River? Or when you took me with you to the 4-H camp where you were the director? I think I was three or four, right?"

She made no indication that she could hear me. No hand squeezes. No murmur. Silence.

The hospice nurse came in to check on her and said quietly, "It won't be long."

Then I remembered how in the fall of 1999, my mother, my daughter Genevieve, and I had taken the ferry to Monhegan Island to visit the one-room school where Mom had been invited to share her experiences teaching in the Appalachian Mountains. Mom was eighty by then. I was sixty, and Genie was thirty. As Genevieve and I watched, Mom told the kids story after story of her teaching years, and we both had wet eyes. Mom still had a sparkle, and she was still working with children. She'd come full circle.

My mind filled with images and smells of Elgood while I sat by Mom's side. Both my mother and I had been reared on the farm by the same parents. We'd done the same chores—milking the cows, gathering the eggs, hoeing the vegetables, picking the fruit, helping Mom Nash with the laundry. In different ways, Mom and Dad Nash had driven both Mom and me forward.

I thought then of all the paths I'd traveled away from Elgood and the farm. I'd become stronger in many ways after I left, but some part of me had always believed I was still trying to find my way back there again. Back to the physical farm itself—the place where I was fully myself.

But I saw now that this idea of home wasn't actually a place I needed to try to return to anymore. The past and the farm had always been with me. So had my parents, and Mom and Dad Nash. I had the deep love and trust of Pebble with me now. I could let Mom go. I was already home, in the true sense of finally knowing myself.

Acknowledgments

Oh dear. Where do I start? This book has been so many years in the writing and so many people have helped and guided me. The first few drafts were put in a drawer for three years while I turned my attention to writing and publishing, *Bill Moss: Fabric Artist & Designer.*

The beginning evolved out of my depression of selling my company that I had run for nearly thirty years. I started getting up at four in the morning to sit in my lounge chair by the fireplace, sipping a cappuccino, with a computer on my lap writing my Morning Pages. Then, through a mutual friend, I met Kathrin Seitz, a writing teacher and coach. Thank you, Kathrin, for seeing potential in my rough work and opening my heart and passion for writing.

The drive to obtain the tools and structure for writing led me to Spalding University in Louisville, Kentucky, for a two-year program to receive my master's degree for creative writing. It was there I met many skillful writers and teachers who were patient and mentored me in shaping my voice. Thank you, Richard Goodman, Diane April, Sena Jeter Naslund, Roy Hoffman, and others in lectures and conversations. This is where I learned to finally say aloud, "I am a writer."

Many thanks to Scott Wolven, Jane Roseman, Jim Rasenberger, Scott Edelstein, and Michele Leavitt, who at various stages edited my work and gave me specific guidance, and from all, I learned a great amount. Scott Edelstein edited and coached me to finally produce a polished manuscript, after many drafts, deletions, and additions.

My appreciation to Genevieve Morgan at Islandport Press who said *Mountain Girl* was a good fit for the Maine publisher. She accepted my manuscript at a time of uncertainties and challenges in the publishing world.

I had started working on another book specifically on the birth of Moss Tents and the ways in which I led the company to be employee-driven and empathetic, a brand of open-door leadership born largely of my childhood growing up on a subsistence farm in Appalachia, where the elemental values of hard work and humility and community were instilled. For this new book project, I started working with Susan Conley, and it soon became clear that this new book needed to be integrated into the existing memoir. With Susan's help, I wove two manuscripts into one, better shaping the arc of the larger story.

And lastly, I thank my husband and Jane English, who stood by me as I moaned and groaned one day and became joyful the next. They never wavered from supporting, editing, commenting, and urging me on when I was ready to give up.

Further, I thank you, my reader, for giving this book a chance, with the hope that you will not only like it but find something that resonates for you here in these stories about facing our fears and daring to do that which most calls us.

About the Author

Marilyn Moss Rockefeller is the author of the book, *Bill Moss: Fabric Artist & Designer*, which won an IPPY Silver Medal, as well as shorter work in publications such as *Orbis, Maine Boats, Homes & Harbors, Espazio,* and *Louisville Literary Review*. She has an MFA in writing from Spalding University.

Widely recognized as a successful and socially responsible business leader, Marilyn cofounded Moss Tent Works with Bill Moss in 1975. She served as president and CEO of Moss Inc. until she sold the company in 2001. She and Moss Inc. won many awards, including the University of Southern Maine's Distinguished Achievement Award. While president of Moss Inc., Marilyn was recognized by New Hope for Women for establishing supportive workplace policies for domestic violence victims.

She also served as chair of the board of trustees at the Center for Maine Contemporary Art. Born and raised in the hills of West Virginia, she now resides with her husband, James Rockefeller, in midcoast Maine.

Photo by Kari Herer